"I'm a big believer in the power of stories. In our bestselling business parable, *The One Minute Manager*, Spencer Johnson and I helped tens of millions achieve success in their personal and professional lives. W. Craig Reed's new book, *Start with Who*, shows business, marketing, and sales professionals how to persuade any client with just twelve bullets and a story. He also discusses the fascinating neuroscience that explains why storytelling is so powerful. Enjoy and use this thought-provoking book!"

–Ken Blanchard, co-author of *The New One Minute Manager* and *Simple Truths of Leadership*

"W. Craig Reed's *Start with Who* represents the next generation beyond Simon Sinek's *Start With Why* and Gartner's *The Challenger Sale*."

–Indy Bains, VP of Marketing, Workday

"*Start with Who* includes concepts that will help you safely challenge the status quo and innovate for the greater good—like storytelling techniques, messaging guide templates, persuasion models, recruiting secrets, and sales enablement tools."

–Mike Paton, former EOS Worldwide Visionary and co-author of the EOS book, *Process!*

"Just like EOS can help a leadership team take their company to the next level, adopting the concepts and recommendations found in *Start with Who* will help you challenge the biggest and best of your competitors."

–Mark O'Donnell, EOS Worldwide Visionary

"*Start with Who* can help SMBs compete with industry giants by using neuroscience-based storytelling to build and increase trust with customers and candidates."

–Steven Doolittle, Chief Revenue
Officer, RemotelyMe

START WITH WITH WHO

HOW SMALL TO MEDIUM BUSINESSES
CAN WIN BIG WITH TRUST AND A STORY

W. CRAIG REED

Post Hill
PRESS

A POST HILL PRESS BOOK

ISBN: 979-8-88845-056-7
ISBN (eBook): 979-8-88845-057-4

Start with Who:
How Small to Medium Businesses Can Win Big with Trust and a Story
© 2024 by Reed Consulting Group, Inc.
All Rights Reserved

Cover design by Conroy Accord

Unless otherwise specified, images are from Dreamstime.com, including images by Gan Hui (p. 45), Alain Lacroix (p. 47), Bachol12345 (p. 57), Peter Hermes Furian (p. 60), and Jaroslav Frank (p. 167).

Graphics on pp. 38, 139, 161, 170, 173, and 208 were created by the author.

Although every effort has been made to ensure that the personal and professional advice present within this book is useful and appropriate, the author and publisher do not assume and hereby disclaim any liability to any person, business, or organization choosing to employ the guidance offered in this book.

No part of this book may be reproduced, stored in a retrieval system, or transmitted by any means without the written permission of the author and publisher.

Post Hill Press
New York • Nashville
posthillpress.com

Published in the United States of America
1 2 3 4 5 6 7 8 9 10

Also by W. Craig Reed

The 7 Secrets of Neuron Leadership
Spies of the Deep
Red November
Terror in Frankfurt
Status-6

Dedicated to my fellow veterans and their families, as many of them have struggled to start or accelerate small businesses. They are truly the "who" we should thank for continuing to serve their country.

CONTENTS

FOREWORD

If you're reading this book, odds are you own or work for a small or medium business (SMB, or entrepreneurial company). If you happen to work at a larger corporate enterprise, your firm may acquire one of these often rapidly growing businesses—or perhaps several—sometime this year.

For anyone who hasn't experienced both types of organizations, it can be difficult to understand just how unique and different large corporations and privately held entrepreneurial companies can be. Perhaps the most glaring difference is how owners, leaders, and employees of these distinct companies *perceive* the safety, security, and stability their companies provide. Owning stock in a publicly traded company or being employed as a leader or an employee at such a firm *feels* safer and more predictable for a lot of people than being similarly involved at an early-stage entrepreneurial company.

Some of this perception is reality—the probability of business failure at a small firm is much higher than at a well-established, well-capitalized corporation. More than 80 percent of businesses fail in their first five years, and only about 10 percent survive beyond year ten. However, most entrepreneurs believe that—despite the risks and challenges—being in complete control of one's own destiny is far more comforting than being a small cog in a large machine, subject to the whims of stock-market fluctuations, unpredictable changes of ownership or strategy, and corporate politics.

While the mainstream media and our elected officials seem to focus on "big business," small, privately held companies are playing an increasingly vital role in the global economy. According to the World Bank, they represent 90 percent of all businesses and employ more than half of all workers worldwide. These small companies may seem like "David" when compared to much larger and more well-established "Goliath" enterprises, but they account for over 40 percent of the gross domestic product (GDP) for most nations.

That means the success of entrepreneurs and their fledgling companies is something *everyone* should care about, not just the determined people who start these companies or help them grow into tomorrow's corporate juggernauts. Federal, state, and local governments should be doing everything they can to help make it easier for small businesses to succeed, but most agencies treat small companies just like larger corporations. As a result, entrepreneurs feel like they need to leap tall buildings, dig deep ditches, and circumvent massive roadblocks to start and run a new venture. There are dozens of forms, filings, fees, and fingers in the pie. It's confusing, expensive, and potentially devastating.

It's also difficult for entrepreneurial companies to compete with bigger companies in the battle to attract and retain top talent. Nearly 60 percent of business owners say finding and recruiting talent is more difficult than trying to find toilet paper during a pandemic. New anti-gig laws make it tougher to hire 1099 contractors, and it's much harder for a small company to *understand* more complex compensation and benefits programs, much less fund and manage them. In recent years, the people shortage has escalated, and the inability to afford a full-time Human Resources (HR) team turns the recruiting process into a nightmare. Finding the right *who* for the right seat is a tall order.

Assuming a small, growing company can navigate these challenges, the key to success is making sure it delivers tremendous value to the right kind of customers, every single day. That may sound simple, but it's not easy. Whether you build products or deliver services, it's really hard to determine exactly who your ideal customers are, what they want, and how to consistently deliver in a way that delights them at a competitive price. It's even harder when you are the only person on your market research, product development, or sales team. This is precisely why so many entrepreneurial ventures fail, and why we (along with our friend and mentor Gino Wickman) believe those who succeed deserve whatever financial and emotional success they achieve.

At the age of twenty-one, Gino Wickman made the decision to embark on his own entrepreneurial journey. Three years later, he stepped into a role at his family's business, a leading real estate sales training company based in Livonia, Michigan. Working with his father, Floyd Wickman, as well as the leadership team, Gino was able to turn the company around after three years and get it running consistently well. After seven years, he and his team decided to sell the organization.

During that journey, Gino accumulated a set of simple concepts and practical tools (assisted by his father, his business mentor Sam Cupp, and several notable business thought leaders) that helped him and his team clarify and simplify the company's vision and get *much* better at executing on that vision. During this phase of his career, Gino also became one of the founding members of the Detroit chapter of EO (Entrepreneurs' Organization) and began sharing some of these tools with fellow members. He quickly discovered a real knack—and passion—for helping entrepreneurs run better businesses and live better lives.

To document and codify what he'd learned, Wickman created the Entrepreneurial Operating System (EOS). His EOS Process, EOS Model, and EOS Toolbox were specifically designed to help small business owners and leaders get a better grip on their businesses, customers, employees, and lives. Companies implementing EOS focus on strengthening the "Six Key Components" of their business—Vision, People, Data, Issues, Process, and Traction. This creates an organization full of people who are crystal clear on the company's vision, executing on that vision with discipline and accountability, and working together as a more cohesive, functional, open, and honest *team*.

After experiencing success with his local network of entrepreneurs, Gino decided to share EOS with the world. He outlined its concepts and proven techniques in his first book titled *Traction*, which paved the way for six more books in the Traction Library that collectively have sold millions of copies. He and his business partner, Don Tinney, also founded EOS Worldwide, a firm dedicated to sharing EOS with the world through its community of more than 550 EOS Implementers around the globe. Together, Gino and his team (including the co-authors of this introduction) have helped more than 20,000 companies implement EOS, with another 150,000 companies using EOS Tools on their own.

***

Start with Who is a book that explores the question that's asked and answered often—and in a myriad of ways—when a leadership team begins implementing EOS. That question is, "Who?"

The first step in strengthening the Vision and People components, for example, is discovering and defining a company's core values. That process begins with *who*. Specifically, "Who are the three people in this organization you'd consider superstars—the folks you'd love to clone because if you had a hundred of them, you'd defeat the competition and maybe conquer the world?" Once a leadership team answers that question, they align around a handful of characteristics or attributes their superstars have in common, and those become the three to seven core values that define the company's culture. When those values are repeated often and consistently used to hire, fire, review, reward, and recognize people, the leaders have created the culture they want.

In addition to answering the *who* question culturally, companies running on EOS work hard to define exactly what they need from a "skills and experience" standpoint. Leadership teams first define the right structure for the organization, clearly define the expectations for each role or "seat" by using an EOS Tool called the Accountability Chart, and then also use several other EOS Tools to attract and retain people who fit the culture and are great at their clearly defined jobs.

Answering the *who* question is also important outside the organization. When strengthening their company's Vision component, leadership teams define a high-level, four-part marketing strategy. The first and most important part of that strategy requires a team to decide *who* their ideal customer is. The answer is referred to as a company's target market. While that may seem like something most successful companies have already agreed upon, many are not clear or aligned around a definitive answer. So, we dig in and define the demographic, geographic, and psychographic profiles of the kind of people or companies who are most likely to become long-term, high-quality business partners. In other words, *who* are your ideal customers/prospects, where are they, and how do they think?

Once a leadership team agrees on its target market, crafting a marketing message (and process, and tactics) becomes much easier. You simply begin investing 100 percent of your *proactive* selling and marketing activities pursuing ideal prospects and 0 percent chasing relationships that are likely to yield little to no value. That creates a much higher return on a company's investment of its precious sales and marketing resources.

The concepts Gino Wickman and his co-authors lay out in the Traction Library are aligned with the wisdom shared in many other business books such as *Good to Great* by Jim Collins, *Start with Why* by Simon Sinek, *The Four Obsessions of an Extraordinary Executive* by Patrick Lencioni, and the book you're reading, *Start with Who* by W. Craig Reed. Throughout the following pages, Reed offers a new, more recent perspective about *who* firms should hire and fire. Also, about *who* we should target and nurture as ideal customers. Most importantly, this book can help us better understand how to effectively communicate with and persuade candidates, employees, prospects, and customers based on the latest behavioral and brain science, as well as provide sage wisdom about persuasion and storytelling. While not exclusively focused on entrepreneurial companies, *Start with Who* is ideal for any business owner, leader, or individual contributor at any size company, as long as they are willing to step out of their comfort zones and take risks.

If you're an executive at a large corporation, reading books like *Traction, Process!*, or *Start with Who* may motivate you to make change happen in a way that moves beyond your firm's safe and secure boundaries. If that seems like a constraint, *Start with Who* includes concepts that will help you safely challenge the status quo and innovate for the greater good—like storytelling techniques, messaging guide templates, persuasion models, recruiting secrets, and sales enablement tools.

If you're at a smaller company, the greater flexibility and appreciation for finding new and better ways of doing things will make these books a perfect accelerant of your desire to change the game for the better. Just like EOS can help a leadership team take their company to the next level, adopting the concepts and recommendations found in *Start with Who* will help you challenge the biggest and best of your competitors.

Having the courage to embrace change can be risky, but it can also be rewarding. Wherever your employment or entrepreneurial journey takes you, we're motivated to help you get everything you want from your business.

***

Mike Paton is an EOS Implementer who succeeded Gino Wickman and spent five years as EOS Worldwide's Visionary. He's the host of the top-rated podcast *The EOS Leader* and co-authored two books in the Traction Library—*Get a Grip* and *Process!*

Mark O'Donnell is the current EOS Worldwide Visionary, former Head Coach and EOS Implementer who has worked with over one hundred companies to help them get what they want from their businesses. He's also a serial entrepreneur who has built and sold multiple entrepreneurial companies like the ones talked about in this book.

CHAPTER 1

VIRTUAL STORMS

John Bettoni's hands shook as he stared at the monitor on his desk. His pulse quickened. One by one the green indicators on the screen blinked, turned yellow, and then red. A Christmas tree gone postal. How had this happened? John tried to remember. Just a few months ago his colleagues were patting him on the back and high-fiving him in the

Seattle data center. At his prompting, the small financial services firm he worked for had authorized the budget required to move forward.

Excited, John's team implemented his grand plan to further consolidate and upgrade. The advantages were clear, the return on investment appeared sound, and the technology was proven. Initial results were promising. They reduced expensive system costs. Management time plummeted and resources were better utilized. Weeks later, things turned sour. An unexpected scenario unfolded, and John had a bad feeling that his days as the director of information technology at Henderson Financial might be numbered.

John had joined Henderson less than a year earlier. His boss, Norman Gage, served as the company's chief information officer. When John was interviewing for his job, Gage had told him the company was a dynamic, high-growth entrepreneurial company in the financial sector. John could leverage his many years of experience and make a difference. But success is always preceded by hard work fraught with risk. Henderson was not a forgiving environment. Mistakes here came with severe consequences. Underperformers never lasted long.

A few months into the job, John made a mistake. It was a minor thing, but it didn't go unnoticed. Gage cornered John in the data center and told him if he messed up again, he should practice saying "French fries or onion rings?" into a microphone. Gage made the comment with a slight smile, like it was a joke, but John had never seen Gage strive for funny.

John had been replaying the memory in his head when Gage came storming into his office. The man's pudgy cheeks were beet red, and his forehead glistened with beads of sweat. His normally brown eyes were bloodshot crimson, as if he were channeling a demon.

Gage crossed John's office in three strides. He stammered when he spoke. Spittle flew off his lips. "What…you…you….what?" His breath reeked of bad coffee. A doughnut crumb clung to his chin.

"I've got it under control," John lied. He hated the lie, but he had a wife and two young daughters to feed. Last week was little Julie's fifth birthday. He'd promised her a new house with her own room someday.

She had hugged him tight, given him a toothless grin, and said all she really wanted for Christmas were her two front teeth. She kissed his cheek and waddled up to bed. John's eyes had filled with tears.

Gage calmed down enough to speak. "You've got one week, Bettoni. Understood? One week before we go live with the new service offerings and all heck breaks loose. If you can't get this fixed by then…"

"I know," John said, "I'll need to learn how to say 'French fries…'"

Gage turned and marched out, cursing, snorting, and shaking his head like a mad bull.

John lowered his head and closed his tired eyes. He searched his worried brain for an answer. He needed help but did not know where to turn. Then he remembered. He opened his eyes and lifted his head, along with his hope. He palmed his mouse and double-clicked on LinkedIn. The web-based professional social network had become the largest in the world with some 850 million members. John had amassed over 1,000 first-level connects and did not know most of them. He had been frequently pinged by hundreds, who used the system's InMail to send unsolicited messages. Most of these were obvious or lightly veiled spam messages that John deleted. He accepted Connect requests from only a few.

Like virtually all his colleagues, he also no longer accepted cold calls and deleted cold emails. He simply did not have time to respond. However, there had been one outreach a few months ago that had intrigued him. The approach had been unique and informative, and the messaging compelling, so John had agreed to connect with this person on LinkedIn. Over the past few months, this professional had communicated unobtrusively, and the content imparted had been timely, thought-provoking, and engaging.

John clicked a few times until he found the person's LinkedIn profile. Her name was Linda Singer, and she worked for a technology solution provider called LeadingDynamics. Originally, she had sent him a Connect request simply stating that she wanted to connect so she could invite him to join an exclusive LinkedIn Group for leaders. Also, to provide him with executive leadership research. This was intriguing to

John and the first time he'd seen someone in sales or marketing offer him leadership development information in this way. John had clicked on Linda's LinkedIn profile and had also found it to be refreshingly different.

While most sales or marketing professionals tended to brag a lot about themselves on their profile, Linda did not. Most profile copy made the person appear to be constantly trolling for a new job, which always raised a red flag in John's mind. Were they content at their current firm? If not, then why not? Were there issues with the management, culture, revenue, or solutions that might cause people to jump ship?

Linda's profile seemed different. She rarely used the term "sales" in her profile. Instead, she used words like colleague, collaborator, expert, strategic partner, servant leader, helpful, or friend. She outlined her core values. Even her title was simply "strategic account manager."

Her profile talked about her passion and purpose, her motivations and areas of expertise and interest. She told short stories about how she had been fulfilled professionally by helping her colleagues (not customers) solve pervasive problems and achieve success. About how she had been rewarded by ensuring others accomplished their goals. She used actual customer quotes along with words and phrases that evoked a friendly, personable tone. John had come away feeling like he'd made a new friend. With many others, he'd been reminded of the movie *Ghostbusters* wherein he felt like he'd been "slimed."

After connecting, Linda had sent John something he'd never seen before: a personalized message that included information about him, his interests, skills, and more. Also, she used words and tone that seemed to resonate with him, as if she had met him before. Linda included a link to a Leadership Profile Survey. Curious, he had clicked. The landing page welcomed him to a short survey that ensured LeadingDynamics sent John relevant, interesting, and personalized thought-leadership information. Also, information on the topic of leadership development that might help with his career advancement. She also sent him a link to a detailed neuroscience-based assessment that included best practices, team development strategies, and a powerful decision-making template. Curious, John clicked on that as well.

The assessment displayed visually interesting and contrasting pictures and videos, along with numeric scales to select the degree to which he related to the videos and images displayed. John had taken personality profiling and career evaluation tests before, but this was quite different and apparently based on the latest science. He answered the questions and within seconds received an email in his inbox. The email contained a link to his assessment. He clicked and downloaded. A minute later, he raised an eyebrow. The assessment seemed incredibly accurate. It outlined his leadership traits, communication style, preferences, and professional attributes. It then recommended best practices and improvements to enhance his leadership abilities and career. John found all this thought-provoking, useful, and unique. It certainly set Linda apart from all the rest.

John also found a link at the bottom of the email that sent him to a company landing page. To his surprise, instead of seeing lots of copy and "here's what we do" messaging, he instead saw a link to a section labeled "Challenges." He clicked on a few that he'd been concerned about. The page portrayed easy to comprehend pictures with minimal text related to various problems, along with short descriptions for each. He found one that seemed relevant and clicked. Again to his surprise, instead of finding a phone book's worth of copy about what the company provided, he'd been directed to a short video. He started the video, which briefly discussed the problem in a questioning style and then ended with a few interesting questions about what he'd viewed. No copy, no downloads, no white papers. John was surprised by the approach.

Based on his preferences and answers to the questions, John occasionally received emails with links to a few thought-leadership documents. None of these contained an overabundance of sales jargon. Most white papers or articles he'd downloaded from other vendors were just smoke screens for a sales pitch. They offered a few tidbits of useful information but then slanted their take to focus on an array of solutions, as if they were a jackknife that could do everything.

The content received from LeadingDynamics broke the mold on this approach. It was well written and engaging without being biased. It usually contained a one-page synopsis so John could decide if it was relevant, and if so, download it. The documents were no more than three or four pages long, used a compelling storytelling approach, and covered important topics from a variety of unbiased angles. The conclusion included a brief mention of LeadingDynamics and their capabilities, but not a glossy sales pitch. He recalled that one of the documents warned of a similar scenario to the one he now faced, as if it had been a prognostication about his current dilemma. He'd found the article quite interesting and had implemented some of the tactics, but he had to admit that he'd not heeded all the advice or contacted Linda for more information. Perhaps he should have. Still, she had not been pushy and instead had continued to send occasional information and point him to various articles or news posts.

John clicked on the Message button on LinkedIn and sent Linda a quick text to contact him about an issue. Linda replied right away that she could call John first thing in the morning. John had a full calendar and so scheduled the call for 1:00 p.m. the following day. John then sent an email to his firm's current solution provider, FisionWorks, even though he had doubts about their ability to help with this situation.

That afternoon, a sales rep named Dwayne Peterson from FisionWorks replied to John's email. John invited him to join a video call, and Dwayne's face popped onto his screen. The mid-thirties district manager had short brown hair and smiling white teeth. John had worked briefly with this partner previously, and the company seemed sound but not stellar.

Dwayne asked what was up. John took a deep breath. He touched a small globe on his desk and spun it around on its spindle. His seven-year-old, Angela, had given him the ornament. She had seen it in a toy store, tugged on her mother's blouse, and said, "Mommy, can we give Daddy the world?"

"How can I help you?" Dwayne prompted, bringing John back to the present.

"I'm having a bad day," John said into his desk camera. "We expanded our virtualization project, consolidated servers, and implemented a cloud storage solution. At first, everything was great. Then we got a few storms. Then some tsunamis."

John hoped Dwayne knew what he meant. Performance slowed when dozens of users tried to access files from various systems at the same time. These "storms," as they were called, were like a dozen people trying to get through the same door at the same time. Tsunamis occurred when the traffic turned into a stampede.

"How slow are we talking?" Dwayne said.

"Slow like my five-year-old reads books slow," John said.

"I see."

"Slow like turtles on sleeping pills slow."

"Interesting picture."

"Slow like I'm going to be waiting in the unemployment line slow," John said.

"That's pretty bad slow," Dwayne said. He smiled and leaned forward. He asked for screen control and then displayed a PowerPoint presentation. "You're in luck, my friend, because FisionWorks has just the right answer for you."

"But I..." John started.

Dwayne waved him off. "Let me show you what I mean."

Dwayne flipped to the first slide in his presentation. "As you can see, FisionWorks is a mega-million-dollar value-added reseller with hundreds of employees, and we've been around for decades and have won dozens of awards and represent some of the largest firms in the industry, including all of the name brands that offer every imaginable solution you could ask for, and we have dozens of trained experts in virtualization and cloud storage solutions and we also offer professional services and assessments and I'm confident we can find a solution to any problem you might have."

Dwayne inhaled a deep breath and then flipped to the next slide. The screen displayed more words than Tolstoy's *War and Peace*. "Here's all the solutions we offer and the vendors we represent." He grinned and waved a hand in the air, as if he were a game show host. He proceeded to name every solution and vendor and described in technical detail every value proposition for every offering of every type. Thirty minutes later, he took another deep breath. "As you can see, there's just no question that we're the right choice to help you solve your problems."

John leaned back in his chair. "Do you know what my problems are?"

"Well, whatever they are," Dwayne said, "I'm sure my technical team can suggest the right solutions to solve them."

John turned his head and starred at the globe on his desk, the one Angela had given him. He wasn't feeling comfortable with Dwayne but figured he should at least go the distance. He needed some answers. John spent the next half hour asking Dwayne dozens of questions. For almost every answer, Dwayne referred to his PowerPoint presentation or a brochure or white paper or some other document. He offered assurances that FisionWorks could do various assessments to uncover the cause of John's problems and provide solutions to resolve them, but he did not impart any new insights or revelations.

John thanked Dwayne for his time and said he'd be in touch. Dwayne promised to email with more information and "touch base" the following day to schedule a call with his technical experts. John nodded and ended the video call.

John spent the rest of the day and much of that evening trying to find some answers to his problems. His wife, Sherry, called twice. She said the girls wanted to know where Daddy was. John said he'd be home soon. By midnight, he was. The house was dark and smelled of pine from the Christmas tree. He tiptoed into the girls' room. Blonde curls draped across tiny pillows. Julie opened one eye. She flashed him a toothless smile and rolled over and snuggled into her pillow. John walked over and kissed her cheek. Her smile broadened. Angela slept nearby. He kissed her cheek too, left the room, and pulled his weary body up the stairs.

Promptly at nine the next morning, John received an email from Dwayne. Attached were a dozen documents, including white papers, customer success stories, vendor brochures, and so forth. Links in the email connected to videos, ROI calculators, and case studies. John browsed through several of them but didn't find anything relevant.

Prior to lunch, Gage marched into John's office and demanded an update. John said he'd contacted a few experts and he would have some answers soon. As Gage stormed off, John hoped that he hadn't just lied to his boss again. By late afternoon, John was beginning to believe that he probably had. He'd made little progress on the issue when his phone chimed. He glanced at his watch and remembered that he'd scheduled a call with Linda Singer.

"Hi, John," Linda said. "You asked me to call you today at one. Is now still a good time?"

"It is," John said. "Thanks for calling."

Linda said, "Your message briefly stated your current problems, so I reviewed these with our technical team. I have a few more questions and several potential concerns. Would you mind if I started with the questions?"

John was impressed that Linda had taken the time to research his issues, and he was intrigued by her mention of "potential concerns." *What concerns?*

"I don't mind," John said. "Please ask away."

"Thank you," Linda said. "I want to be as helpful as possible. I sensed in the tone of your message that your issues are urgent, and I'd like to help you resolve these before they cause any internal problems with your team or management."

John did not respond as he thought about Gage's red face.

Linda continued, "First, please take a moment to explain in detail the issues you're currently having."

John explained.

"Thanks," Linda said. "What I heard is that you recently expanded your virtualization footprint and are now having virtual storm performance issues. Is that correct?"

"Yes, big-time."

"Are you also experiencing any security issues or incompatibilities?"

John raised an eyebrow. "Not as yet, but it's always a potential concern. For now, we've been focused on the performance issues."

"Which applications are the slowest?" Linda asked.

"Mostly our legacy and business apps."

"What's your physical server to virtualized machine count?"

John was again impressed. Rarely did a vendor ask him this question. John gave her the answer.

"How many terabytes on your storage area network?"

Again, John gave her the information.

"How many desktops have you virtualized?" Linda asked. Her voice sounded pleasant, confident, and professional.

"About a hundred so far," John said.

"I see," Linda said. "We've helped hundreds of firms like yours across several decades, and we often see bottleneck issues like these. This is because your virtual machines reside on your servers, but your data—all the employee files and so forth—resides on your storage. When users try to access that data, a bottleneck can occur. Fortunately, our technical experts have solved similar issues with simple, fast, and affordable solutions, so that's not what concerns me."

John raised both eyebrows. "Then what is?"

"I noticed that you operate in ten US states. Is that correct?"

"Yes. Is that relevant?"

"Yes, very relevant, as I'll explain."

"Okay," John said as he swallowed hard. Sweat lined his palms.

"Your answers indicated that you've moved lots of data to the cloud. Is that correct?"

"Yes," John said. "I figured we could move some files to the cloud and save on local storage costs."

"That's a smart move," Linda said, "but as you know, many cloud solutions can be less than secure and slow. Unfortunately, many of them are software-based, and that makes it easier for bad guys to steal your data."

"The solution I implemented is software-based, and they assured me it was secure. Are you saying it's not?"

Linda's voice turned urgent. "Yes, precisely. I'm sure you've heard of the recent Headstart Bug? It's a flaw with software security that allows hackers to steal sensitive information. That's a bad enough problem on its own, but now it's even worse due to recent updates in most US state civil codes. I assume you're storing personal information for your customers in the ten states you operate in?"

John sat forward in his seat. "Well, yes, of course we are. What's the problem?"

"If you're hacked and can't prove you properly protected the information, your firm could be fined and forced to publicly disclose the breach, but that's not the worst of it."

John bit his lip. "What is?"

Linda's tone became even more urgent. Her sentences had a short, staccato quality. "Most state codes also allow for a 'private cause of action.' This action will come from your customers. They can now more easily sue you. The combined lawsuits could cost your firm millions."

John's heart fluttered. His virtual storm performance issues were bad enough, but now things had taken a turn for the worse. How was he going to explain to Gage that by moving to the cloud, he had exposed the company to millions in potential fines and lawsuits? If his job was on the line before, it was hanging by a thread now. "Are there any answers to this problem?"

Linda's voice sounded calm, assuring, and comforting. "Fortunately, yes. There is a logical solution. There's an 'Encryption Safe Harbor' clause for all civil codes that can protect you if the right actions are taken. How are you encrypting your data?"

"We're relying on the encryption provided by the cloud vendors."

"I was afraid of that," Linda said, sounding concerned again. "They might not meet all the requirements. You may be exposed to potential fines or lawsuits."

"Just what I wanted to hear," John said as he snapped a pencil in two.

"Are you working with anyone to help you solve these issues, John?"

"I contacted another partner, and they're researching answers now."

"Did they inform you of the consequences for violating these codes?"

"No."

"Well, even so," Linda said, "I suspect you're in good hands and probably would not entertain a second opinion at this point. I hope I've at least been of some help and would be happy to answer any questions you might have in the future."

John was puzzled. Every other sales professional he'd spoken with during his career had always pushed for a follow-on call. He figured the action had been drilled into them by their sales managers. Why wasn't Linda asking him for a meeting?

"You said your team had solved problems like the one I'm having," John said. "I'd like to know more about that. I'd also like to learn more about these civil codes."

"I don't want to interfere with anyone you might already be working with," Linda said.

"I haven't signed any agreements, and I'm only at the research stage, so there's no issues."

"If that's the case, then I'd be happy to schedule a video call with my technical team to do a no-cost review of your infrastructure to determine why you're having performance issues, and also discuss ways to ensure your security conforms to the various civil codes. They're open tomorrow afternoon or Thursday morning. Which is best for you?"

"The sooner the better. Let's do tomorrow."

"Done. I'll email you an invitation, and I'll also send you a summary about the civil codes so you can review this information prior to the meeting. In addition, I'll send you a two-page Critical Tech Alert about your virtual storm issue. I think you'll find both very informative."

"Thanks," John said. "I look forward to the call."

Minutes later, John received an invite and a separate email from Linda. It contained a brief overview of various civil codes in the body of the email and an attached PDF document. Also, a web link. John read through the information. He then completed an internet search and discovered that everything Linda had said was accurate. He frowned. He'd dropped a big ball by not finding out about these state civil codes prior to implementing a cloud solution that could have security gaps. Fortunately, Linda had brought this to his attention in time to solve the issue before Gage found out.

John opened the email attachment. The headline read "Critical Tech Alert." Unlike the typical white paper or solution brief, this focused on a single issue that firms might see. Nearly every other vendor document John had read offered a few paragraphs on a problem before drowning you with a fire hose on solutions and company accolades. This CTA document did the opposite. It explained in detail, without getting verbosely technical, how bottlenecks can cause performance storms like the one John's firm had experienced. John was encouraged. The document did not provide much detail on solutions but instead briefly discussed three potential courses of action. The CTA intimated that only a full assessment could determine which of the three actions might be the most logical choice.

John felt a glimmer of hope. If these guys were this versed with the problem, then maybe, just maybe, they could recommend a solution. So far, John had been intrigued by Linda's unique approach, as well as her preparation, research, and thought-leadership knowledge. Now, he hoped that might translate into some solid answers that could help him keep his job.

CHAPTER 2
HITTING THE TARGET

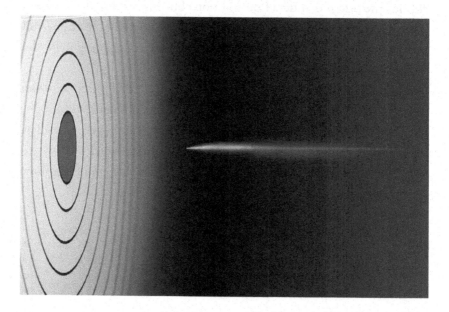

In the LeadingDynamics field office, Linda Singer studied the information John Bettoni had given her. After her call with John, she had updated his profile in the company's Customer Relationship Management system and reviewed the Communications Trust Playbook she'd received after John had completed the professional assessment she had sent him. It offered keen insights into his motivations, fears, demeanor, sales triggers, and leadership style. For Linda, it was like having a flashlight and a road map to help understand who John was, why he might care about something, how to adjust her sales messaging accordingly, and how to build trust. But Linda also understood that with great knowledge came even greater responsibility.

Linda glanced at a framed picture resting on the left side of her desk. Therein, her family beamed smiles at an unseen camera. Her husband, Bob, and her two sons, Joey and Tommy, stood by her side. She knew her smile was genuine and not just painted on for the moment. She also knew it would not, *could* not be that way if she had not learned several valuable lessons.

Earlier in her career, Linda had occasionally used customer insights and knowledge to manipulate, coerce, or cajole a customer into buying. Like all junior salespersons, she had been under immense pressure to perform and hit her numbers. She also recalled a few times where she had cut corners or told her customers white lies to get a purchase order. She was not proud of these missteps in her career, but she had learned from them and was now committed to maintaining a different course ruled by integrity and honesty.

Months ago, when Linda had engaged with John as part of an account-based marketing campaign, John had clicked on the link in the LinkedIn message Linda had sent. He had answered the assessment questions, and his customer record had been automatically updated to include the Playbook. Linda now had a much clearer picture of John's world and who he was, but not just in the traditional terms of Budget, Authority, Need, and Timing. Linda understood well that the age-old BANT formula was "oh so nineties" and far too inadequate for today's remote selling environment.

Almost no customer Linda had engaged with over the past five years could articulate an accurate budget figure. If asked this question, they all said they had zero budget. However, Linda had found that if the pains or needs were great enough, customers could always find budgets. As for authority, new research from leading analyst firms validated that more than a dozen individuals could be involved in a typical business sale, and any one of them could have the "authority" to say yay or nay along the way. Many of them could play the role of a decision-maker, influencer, or gatekeeper at any point in the sale. As for timing, Linda knew it was her responsibility to create a strong enough sense of urgency to make the timing immediate.

Linda did not assume that the person's title translated to "decision-maker." She always asked questions regarding the prospect's current authority as related to her solutions. These questions were designed to uncover whether her contact was an influencer and therefore not authorized to make a final decision. If so, this altered the type of questions she asked and how she asked them. Closing an influencer on a final sale was not feasible, but gaining help from this person to understand the inner workings of the organization—including the organizational chart and decision-making process—could be of great benefit. Linda's objective with an influencer was to close this person on gaining their help to get an audience with others who could make decisions.

An evaluator also did not have final decision-making authority but was usually responsible for evaluating, reviewing, or implementing a solution. They often narrowed the selection down to three final vendors, then kicked the tires until a winner emerged. Linda's goal with this role player was to impart concerning thought-leadership information in the form of at least one unknown urgent risk they were not aware of.

Using the Communications Trust Playbook had helped Linda accomplish this and made the age-old BANT formula obsolete. In today's selling environment, this was better phrased as ACTS.

The A stands for "adequate." Few prospects believed they had critical or urgent fires they needed squelched. Most were like frogs in warm water and believed their current situation was adequate. Linda needed to use research and thought-leadership information to inform them about unknown urgent risks. If this information did not start to "boil the frog's water" and at least spur a few concerns, Linda raised a mental yellow flag. Finding a budget might be difficult if not impossible for something considered less than critical. This was often a signal for Linda to change paths and sell in a different direction or write off the account as unqualified.

The C stands for "concerned." This is how the prospect needed to feel after a conversation with Linda. While she still probed for needs and concerns the customer was aware of, she knew these were rarely sufficient to motivate immediate action. By informing the prospect about potential risks, Linda became a reliable source of information and a trusted advisor to help customers avoid potential pitfalls. If she could make customers aware of a large enough pain or risk, she could boil their water and move them out of comfort zones.

Linda knew that her greatest competitor was usually "Mr. Do Nothing," who would always win unless doing nothing appeared riskier or more difficult than doing the right thing. For John Bettoni, she had used thought-leadership information about state civil codes related to security to elevate his concerns about risk and increase motivation to take immediate action. This was the T, which stands for "tense." Often overlooked by many sales professionals, Linda saw this as the most important step. She needed to raise the stakes in the game by raising the tension. If the prospect did not believe there might be an immediate risk, he or she might be unlikely to take action.

The S stands for "satisfied." Linda's goal with any engagement was to ensure the prospect walked away satisfied. She offered three logical choices to avoid the consequences of nonaction. If the prospect was not yet convinced to move forward, it did not mean the sale was lost. Often, the prospect needed more time and convincing before they could be satisfied with the decision to purchase.

Linda never asked a question like, "When do you plan to implement a solution?" If the customer was not even aware of the risks she had revealed, how could they answer this question? She found it far more advantageous to ask about impending deadlines, such as project completions, merger dates, senior management mandates, and so forth.

Linda stood from her desk and stared out the window of her office. A dozen floors below, at a busy intersection, a line of vehicles lurched forward when the light turned green. Moments later, another sea of cars ground to a halt when the light turned red. It had taken Linda many years, but with the help of a mentor, she had learned how to stop trying to force solutions or control people, places, or things.

Her mentor's name was Sridhar, who had enjoyed an illustrious and successful business career and now wished only to help others. With calm confidence and patient understanding, he had taught her to become more in tune with life's traffic lights and to slow, stop, or go when the time was right. By letting go of all the outcomes she could never control anyway, and ceasing to fight the currents by swimming upstream, Linda had found an abundance of joy and wealth.

Linda took another sip of coffee and returned to her desk. She looked at her monitor and again studied the Communications Trust Playbook. The web page listed John's primary attributes as a helpful leader. The Playbook also revealed John's typical mannerisms and a profile overview about his likely team interactions. This helped Linda understand how John might interface with his team and delegate responsibilities. Numerous keywords noted in the Playbook had helped Linda align her messaging with John's during their initial conversation. For example, words like helpful, adaptable, sensitive, nurturing, caring, and relationships would resonate well with John, and she had used several during her call with him.

The Playbook also provided John's primary fears and motivators, and Linda understood well that these should never be manipulated but instead understood so she could sincerely help John solve his problems. Also in the Playbook were more than a dozen DOs and DON'Ts she should implement or avoid to ensure a congenial relationship with John.

Over the past few years, Linda had found these Playbooks invaluable in establishing a close professional relationship with her customers. This was contrary to what she'd learned previously when she'd studied *The Challenger Sale*, where she'd read there were five types of salespeople and that a Relationship Builder was the least successful. Instead, the authors admonished that she should be a more assertive Challenger salesperson by challenging her customer's belief systems. While she agreed with this approach at the right time in the sale, she had nevertheless found it nearly impossible to shed her skin and become something, or someone, she was not. By first building a relationship, she established trust. Only then could she challenge by offering a different point of view.

Virtually all sales models she'd tried were "one size fits all." A few outlined a buyer profile based on observational data and recommended some sales tricks, but none used solid science to create an easy-to-use framework. While these had not worked well for her in the past, the approach she used today had proved invaluable. Armed with the right tools, messaging, and information, Linda could now enjoy a deep, restful night's sleep before her meeting in the morning with John.

The following day, John connected with Linda on a video call. Smiling broadly, she held up a cup of coffee and asked if he wanted one. John laughed, held up his own cup in front of the camera, and said he was one step ahead. Steam drifted from the cup and filled John's nose with the scent of Italian dark roast. Another face appeared on the monitor and introduced himself as Steve Tully, a sales engineer at LeadingDynamics.

Linda asked, "How do your employees feel about the performance problems you're having? Are these issues affecting your professional relationships?"

"Do you remember the movie *Airplane*?" John said.

"Vaguely," Linda said with a smile.

"There's a scene where most of the passengers line up with wrenches, knives, and pipes while waiting to pummel the protagonist for messing up. That's what it's like outside my office these days."

Linda laughed. "Obviously some fair-weather fans. How about your boss?"

John cringed and said nothing.

Linda cocked her head to one side. "That bad?"

"Yup."

"I understand. A friend of mine lost his job years ago due to a similar issue. That was before we knew enough about this problem to offer him some helpful options."

"Let's hope it doesn't come to that," John said.

"I'm confident it won't," Steve said. "As Linda mentioned, we do care about your circumstance and can recommend three actions we can take to help solve your problems. Let's determine which one is the most logical choice for you."

The three of them spent the next hour analyzing performance logs, studying reports, reviewing data, and using the video system's whiteboard. They drew diagrams, batted around theories, and explored potential culprits. Steve concluded by saying they'd collected enough information and he needed to take this back to his team for analysis.

"Not to worry," Linda said. "We'll reconnect in a few hours with some answers for you, but before then, I have a few more questions."

John forced a smile and nodded. "Ask away."

Linda asked John several more questions about the criticality of solving the issues they had uncovered, along with the risks he had not previously known that Linda had revealed—further exposing his firm to security risks related to state civil codes. She also asked about the decision-making process and who was involved at various stages. As for his needs, these were obviously clear, but Linda asked about other areas of need that could be affected by the situation they were currently dealing with. John was appreciative of these questions, as they seemed designed to ensure that economies of scale could be leveraged, but also to avoid unintended consequences if the wrong solutions were implemented.

Finally, Linda asked about John's sense of urgency. While in John's mind this was abundantly obvious, Linda asked several intelligent questions about how she and LeadingDynamics could speed things along by helping to smooth the purchasing process in advance. Linda concluded the conversation, and she and Steve disappeared from the call. For the first time in a long time, John allowed himself to cling to a glimmer of hope. Maybe he'd still have a job on Christmas Day.

That afternoon, Linda and Steve reconnected with John on a video call, and Linda began by delivering some bad news. "I know you're probably not ready to implement any solutions, but we've found some things that concern us. Steve will explain."

John squirmed in his seat.

Steve shared his screen and displayed a spreadsheet. "We figured out what's going on." He used his mouse to point to some figures. "It's all about your system 'chops,' which is a technical term." Steve smiled. "You don't have enough to handle the storms, let alone the tsunamis."

"But I ran tests and didn't see any issues," John said.

Steve nodded. "Unfortunately, most tests only give you a glimpse at any point in time or across a small portion of your potential problem areas. The best way to determine your total requirement is to calculate it like this." Steve again used his mouse to point at an area on the screen. He went through the estimation in detail while showing various charts and graphs. "Now let's talk about your storage," Steve said.

"Our storage?"

"You made the right decision going to a high-performance one," Steve said.

"I figured," John said. "I wanted to avoid that proverbial problem like a dozen people trying to go through a small door at the same time."

"Your performance is good, but it may not be enough," Steve said as he pointed to a diagram on his screen. He explained why slow performance could be causing John's issues.

"Turtles," John said.

"Turtles," Linda echoed.

"You've also got another problem," Steve said. "Your servers also may not have enough chops."

"I don't have the budget to buy any more," John said.

"We understand," Linda said, "but you're going to need to replace some of your slower turtles with ones that have more oomph."

"Oomph?" John said.

"It's also a technical term," Linda said with a smile. "It means chops."

"Thanks for explaining," John said with a smile. "So aside from buying more servers, which I can't afford, what's the answer? I'm on a short leash here."

"We'd first like to validate our numbers," Linda said, "and if they're correct, then we've narrowed it down to three logical choices. The first one is to do nothing, which I'm sure you'll agree carries far too much risk."

"I do agree," John said. "What are the other two choices?"

Linda said, "Choice number two is to buy more systems, which we assume you can't afford."

"Correct. I definitely don't have the budget for that choice."

"Choice number three is not only affordable," Linda said, "but it should solve your problems."

John cocked an ear. "I'm listening."

Steve explained the third option in detail while pointing to a few diagrams on the screen. The graphics were simple, clear, and the page was not cluttered with lots of copy.

"I like the sound of that," John said. "But what about my security issues?"

Linda said, "We've outlined three logical choices for that as well. Choice one is, of course, to do nothing. We assumed that this choice was unacceptable."

"You assumed correctly," John said.

Linda nodded, explained choice two, and then said, "We figured this option would also be unacceptable."

"Again," John said, "you are correct."

Steve used another diagram to explain choice three and concluded by saying, "This might be the most logical choice, given the low total cost of ownership."

John raised an eyebrow. "So I simply replace the solution I have now with this one and, voilà, problem solved?"

"Yes," Steve said. "However, you'll need to upgrade a few other items, but we can help with that."

John wrinkled his nose. "I don't know. We invested a lot in the solutions we have, and I don't want to tell my boss I made a bad decision."

Linda said, "To clarify, I believe the question you're asking is, 'How can you economically justify replacing your current solution with a better one?' Is that correct?"

"Yes, exactly," John said.

"I understand how you feel," Linda said. "Others have felt this way, and Steve will explain how they answered that question."

Steve's mouse hovered over a return on investment calculator on the screen. "This ROI calc shows how you can eliminate several cost areas that will allow you to reach breakeven within six months and then gain a cost avoidance going forward. As you can see, the answer to your question is that it actually makes more financial sense to replace some of your current solutions with more reliable, secure, and efficient ones."

John studied the numbers while nodding. "I'll need you to fully explain this to my boss and to the CFO."

"Absolutely," Steve said. Let's show you how another firm implemented this solution, and the results they experienced."

"Good," John said. "I don't want to be a guinea pig."

Linda took control and displayed a customer success story using a storytelling approach. Page one used one picture and three bullet points to introduce a customer decision-maker and describe his situation. Linda briefly discussed the customer's business and laid the foundation for the decision-maker's problems.

In the next slide, which also contained only one graphic and three bullets, Linda outlined the customer's problems, and in the next slide she showed how, if ignored, they could have led to serious consequences. The customer unsuccessfully tried a few solutions, but they did not resolve the issues. In some cases, they made the situation worse. In the final slide, again containing one pic and three bullets, Linda described how the customer had three choices: do nothing and drive off the proverbial cliff, select a solution similar to the ones that had not previously worked, or explore a new course of action. Aided by LeadingDynamics, and using the most logical choice, the customer solved his problems in time and gained excellent results and management accolades.

John let out a slow breath. He was encouraged by this story, but still harbored doubts.

Linda leaned forward and smiled. "I understand how you feel, and I sincerely want to help. All of us are faced with choices almost every week that could either help or end our careers. I made a decision years ago that I would never recommend something to anyone that I wouldn't be thrilled with myself. I knew that if I wasn't sincere, sooner or later my insincerity would catch up to me. That said, given what we've just learned, you now have less time than before."

John's eyes widened. "I do?"

"Yes," said Steve. "Because of your system limitations, the tsunamis you've been experiencing are escalating and will soon cause a complete shutdown. The downtime consequences could be quite expensive."

"Not to mention career ending," John said as he lowered his eyes.

Linda said, "I recommend we have Steve run a few more tests ASAP to validate his findings, and in the meantime, you and I can discuss the financial arrangements."

John's demeanor reflected determination. "I agree. Let's proceed."

"Excellent," Linda said. "Steve will finalize his tests while you and I review some total cost of ownership figures."

While Steve left the call to run more tests, Linda worked with John to create a total cost of ownership and return on investment analysis that outlined how he could replace several systems that were approaching end of life with newer and more efficient ones.

Linda then demonstrated how the new systems could also cut John's power and energy costs in half. She went through the TCO analysis line by line. Given reduced costs and other efficiencies, the payback could come in less than nine months. Moreover, John could lease the new equipment at an affordable cost from his operating expense budget rather than his capital expense budget.

Steve returned to the call and reported that his initial calculations were not far off. The good news was they had isolated and confirmed the culprits. He recommended a course of action that could solve the problems and prevent any consequences. Before ending the call, Linda showed John an ARC to help him remember how to explain to Gage why they needed to transition from something bad, risky, and costly to something excellent, safe, and affordable. She explained that

ARC stands for "attainable results chart." This simple but powerful chart would help John prepare for his meeting with Gage and ensure approval. She noted that none of it contained vendor names or information, which would appear biased when shown to others. The ARC included information and illustrative icons to depict a before and after scenario.

ARC:

FROM: *Unsecure cloud software encryption that exposes the company to security risks*

TO: *Hardware encryption cloud solution that eliminates security risks*

WHY: *To ensure compliance with US state civil codes and mitigate fines and lawsuits*

HOW: *Fast, simple, painless migration aided by professional services*

WHAT: *Affordable hardware encryption cloud solution with a nine-month ROI*

Confident they'd done all they could to prepare John for his meeting, Linda concluded the call and promised to check back first thing in the morning.

Later that day, after Linda and Steve had departed, John practiced delivering to Gage the information Linda had provided on the ARC. He then prayed that his boss would approve everything. A few hours later, John reviewed the proposal with Gage. His boss's eyes darted back and forth as he examined all the numbers and information. John's throat went dry.

Finally, Gage looked up and said, "I'll talk to the CFO to release the funds you need. But if this doesn't work…"

John swallowed a lump and thanked his boss. He returned to his office, hopeful that the solution would work and he'd be able to keep his job.

Over the next few days, he and the team from LeadingDynamics implemented the changes. With his career at stake, John more than once felt his shoulders knot with stress. At night, Sherry tried to console him, but there was little she could do. A week went by without a single storm or tsunami, but they still needed to provide Gage with a full set of test reports before he'd be convinced they'd solved the issues.

The fateful Monday arrived, and John's hands gripped his steering wheel as he drove into work.

Linda and Steve connected on a video call at 10:00 a.m. John displayed the logs and test results on the screen. First Steve smiled, then Linda. Finally, John let his shoulders relax. He smiled and then grinned. The overall performance improvement exceeded 80 percent. Angry employees no longer lined up outside John's door or lit up his phone line. He did not need to pray every night that hackers wouldn't steal or expose the firm's sensitive information. John was pleased with the results, but now he had to hope Gage didn't have a different opinion.

Two days went by, and John did not hear a word from his boss. He didn't know if that was a good sign or a bad one. At 11:00 a.m. on the third day, one week before Christmas, Gage entered John's office. Two people entered as well and stood near the door. A man and a woman. The CEO and CFO of the company. Gage's face seemed hard, but then again, it always did. Gage approached John's desk. John's heart raced as he stood. If this was bad news, he preferred to take it standing.

"Mr. Bettoni," Gage said.

John tried to answer, but a lump in his throat held his tongue.

The corners of Gage's mouth turned up ever so slightly. "Congratulations." Gage brought forth a plaque. "This is an award from the company for your recent outstanding performance."

John's jaw dropped as Gage handed him the plaque.

"And this," Gage said, handing John an envelope, "is a bonus check for helping save the company money."

John finally let himself smile. The CEO and CFO smiled and nodded approval, and Gage invited John to join the rest of the company in the cafeteria for a Christmas celebration.

That evening, after dinner, John sat near the fireplace and watched the Christmas tree lights sparkle. Angela sat in his lap, with Julie and Sherry nearby.

Angela said, "Daddy, do you still like the globe we got you?"

"Absolutely," John said. "I keep it on my desk where I can see it every day."

"That's good," Angela said with a grin. "We wanted you to have the world."

John's heart filled with joy. He smiled and said, "I already do."

***

Linda Singer smiled as she pressed send. A whoosh sound verified the email had been delivered. Less than a month after helping John Bettoni solve his technical issues and keep his job, she had helped him explore a new one. During her career, she had personally been subjected to the wrath of a bad boss or intolerable co-workers. Eventually, she had realized it was not always their fault. More often, she simply wasn't the right person for that seat.

Having witnessed John's stress and difficult environment, she had recommended he explore an opportunity with another firm that might be a better fit. This company understood that focusing on people rather than only profit led to more productivity, and therefore more profit. They had adopted a business framework called the Entrepreneurial Operating System (EOS), which advised ensuring they had the right people in the right seats. John interviewed with the team, resonated with the company's core values, and decided to accept an offer as chief information officer. Linda had just responded to John's email wherein he'd thanked her and said he was now thriving in his new role.

Linda again glanced out the window at the traffic lights below. One turned green to allow the traffic to flow.

"Right on schedule," she whispered.

CHAPTER 3
THE LANDSCAPE

"By working faithfully eight hours a day, you may
eventually get to be boss and work 12 hours a day."
—Robert Frost

n 2011, author and speaker Simon Sinek started a global movement that inspired millions to ask a simple question: Why? His book and TED Talk series, titled *Start with Why*, seek to answer why some organizations and individuals are more influential, innovative, and persuasive than others. Why some drive higher loyalty from employees, followers, or customers.

Many reviewers have found Sinek's book lacking deep research, but nearly all agree the concepts were inspiring. Sinek reveals that while Martin Luther King Jr., Steve Jobs, and the Wright Brothers had little in common, they all started with the concept of Why. They all came to the same realization: persuading someone to buy into a concept, ideal, solution, or movement must start with an understanding of Why.

Start with Why examines how certain leaders have exerted influence by thinking, acting, and communicating in similar fashion to define the reasons why someone should care about something. Sinek shows how successful firms and individuals start with this concept and then move on to explore the How and What. Many sales, marketing, recruiting, and business professionals have embraced this concept and now begin by asking *why* customers, candidates, or colleagues should care about a solution, profession, or vision before explaining how it will work and what it is.

However, most top sales, marketing, and business professionals know that the reasons why one person might be motivated to take action could be quite different from the reasons why someone else does.

Also in 2011, authors Matthew Dixon and Brent Adamson published *The Challenger Sale: Taking Control of the Customer Conversation*. They based this groundbreaking book on research initiated in 2009 by Corporate Executive Board (CEB), later acquired by Gartner, Inc. The book quickly became a "selling bible" used by millions of sales professionals and referenced by almost as many marketers and corporate executives. In fact, it practically became required reading for anyone involved in customer conversations.

The information and recommendations presented by Dixon and Adamson in the book did not necessarily dispel the research completed by Professor Neil Rackham two decades earlier that led to his book, *SPIN Selling*. In fact, Rackham wrote the foreword to *The Challenger Sale* and conceded that while the research and findings he documented in *SPIN Selling* were still valid, "purchasing has gone through a major revolution." In other words, things have changed a lot since Rackham, Sandler, Miller, and Heiman wrote their books in an era predating the internet, social selling, remote work, and modern neuroscience.

Likewise, more than a decade has passed since CEB conducted its research on thousands of salespersons and almost one hundred companies. Rackham praised this body of work and said the "research has all the initial signs that it may be game-changing." Indeed, by all appearances, it has been. Salespersons around the world are more often teaching, tailoring, and taking control of the sale. This thought-provoking body of research has had a profound impact on the world of selling.

Start with Who does not necessarily dispel the research in *Start with Why* or *The Challenger Sale*. Just as Rackham noted that his original concepts were sound but dated by 2009, Simon Sinek and the authors of *The Challenger Sale* will hopefully be as gracious in conceding that dramatic changes to the business, recruiting, selling, and marketing landscape over the past dozen or more years have made many of their conclusions and recommendations potentially out of date. Some of the most profound paradigm shifts that have occurred in recent years include:

Remote Work

The global pandemic changed the way we work, hire, sell, and market, perhaps forever. By 2025, over thirty-six million Americans will be working remotely (Upwork, 2020). That's an 87 percent increase from pre-pandemic levels. Many sales pros always worked from home, including those in insurance and similar fields. However, according to research by SPOTIO, outside and in-person selling accounted for more than 70 percent of all sales in the US prior to the pandemic. Today, that's flipped. Research from HubSpot revealed that 63 percent of sales leaders say virtual sales meetings are as effective or more so than traditional face-to-face meetings. They're definitely less expensive. No more $500 bottles of cabernet while entertaining prospects.

Any doubt about the future of remote selling was dispelled by McKinsey when they published research on the topic validating that 75 percent of business-to-business (B2B) customers prefer remote sales interactions over traditional face-to-face meetings. Likewise, while some firms have insisted on a return to the office, most have conceded that remote or hybrid work are here to stay. This has opened the door to far different approaches to talent acquisition and employee development.

Account-Based Marketing

Remote work and selling has changed the way marketers do account-based marketing (ABM). Although many of us have been using this approach for the past decade or longer, ABM catapulted to tip-of-tongue fame several years ago and is now touted as a marketing must-have. This strategy dictates a more personalized approach to penetrating target accounts and providing content individualized to specific personas within those accounts. The term seems to imply that it's strictly a marketing discipline, but proper ABM tactics dictate a vastly different framework for remote or hybrid selling. To be effective, ABM requires personalized "just-in-time" content and sales enablement, and that mandates a fundamental change to the typical business approach discussed in *Start with Why* and the sales approach proffered by *The Challenger Sale* or almost any other framework. The advent of artificial intelligence (AI) such as ChatGPT offers the ability to personalize emails and messages on the fly; however, it requires time and knowledge to properly instruct or prompt ChatGPT or similar AI systems to avoid "bad in equals bad out" results.

Neuroscience

Neither Simon Sinek nor the authors of *The Challenger Sale* used the word "neuroscience" in their books. This is understandable, as the science was nascent back then. Today, due to its unprecedented success, neuromarketing has increased exponentially at global firms like Google, Yahoo, Apple, HP, Frito-Lay, Procter & Gamble, and Coca-Cola. Originally embraced by business-to-consumer (B2C) companies, its meteoric results have also been documented by B2B firms. Any salesperson or marketer who does not understand or use neuroscience to personalize communications and content may be at a severe disadvantage to those who do. They risk traversing roads far less illuminated and far more treacherous without the aid of a flashlight or a map into who might resonate with their messaging, and why.

Storytelling

Marketing and sales professionals who do not use *proper* storytelling may not be aware of research completed by Harvard University, leading neuroscientists, and a team of experts at the London Business School. Studies show that most of us forget 90 percent of what we've been taught or told within thirty days. However, if delivered in a proper storytelling format, retention increases by an astounding 1400 percent. Also, proper storytelling can increase the brain chemical responsible for trust, and every great salesperson knows that 90 percent of customers buy on trust. Some sales and marketing professionals may be good storytellers, but they often do so intuitively. They usually have little to no storytelling training but are gifted at "playing it by ear." When formally taught proper storytelling techniques that include plotting, pacing, characterization, setting, vocal tone, and neurolinguistics, even new and under-performing professionals can become home run hitters.

Nancy Duarte published her excellent book, *Resonate*, in 2010—a year before *The Challenger Sale*. Also groundbreaking, Duarte leveraged age-old storytelling techniques and more visual components to create and deliver presentations. While her sage advice is still sound and her workshops are still full, the VisualStories framework is now also potentially outdated. It does not include the latest neuroscience—such as the impact color, vocal tones, or certain words can have on specific brain centers. Also, it does not align with popular sales frameworks, such as *The Challenger Sale* et al., which makes it difficult for sales teams to adopt. Lastly, and perhaps most importantly, it does not quite align with storytelling approaches used by *New York Times* bestselling authors—who are arguably the world's best storytellers.

LinkedIn Social Selling

Launched in 2002, growth at LinkedIn was slow at first—only about twenty sign-ups per day. By 2009, the year CEB did much of its research for *The Challenger Sale*, Jeff Weiner joined LinkedIn as CEO and membership took off. By 2011, when CEB published their book, 90 million members had signed on to LinkedIn. By then, *Start with Why* and *The Challenger Sale* were in print, but the global impact of this giant social network was not yet fully understood. Today, LinkedIn is *the* site for professional networking with around 850 million members worldwide. Any recruiter, salesperson, or marketer not using personalized Social Selling on LinkedIn, or trying to use obsolete tactics for Ads, InMails or Connects, risks mediocre results and lost opportunities to those who are embracing this medium properly.

Leadership Change Management

Implementing any idea, concept, framework, or recommendation within an organization, especially a large one, will not be easy. Executive leadership must embrace these changes and inspire organizational teams to implement them. Many years ago, Ken Blanchard taught us how to be better leaders in his outstanding book titled *The One Minute Manager* (later updated to *The New One Minute Manager*). Blanchard has since co-written several excellent books discussing how we should embrace the concept of servant leadership and adapt our styles to varied situations. My first introduction to leadership training, decades ago, was based on Blanchard's *Situational Leadership* book and training courses, which set the tone for my entire career. Today, the Ken Blanchard Companies offer a course covering change management that I recommend all organizations consider. Simply reading a book such as this one, or Sinek's *Start with Why*, is not enough. Changing the heart and mind of one business leader, marketer, or salesperson is a good start, but the spark will never ignite a fire within an organization if Blanchard's concepts about servant leadership, situational leadership, and change management are not adopted by all involved.

Entrepreneurial Operating System (EOS)

In the foreword to this book, EOS Visionaries Mike Paton and Mark O'Donnell described Gino Wickman's vision to create EOS, now in use by over 170,000 companies around the globe. During EOS Worldwide's formative years, *Traction* author Gino Wickman served as the company's Visionary, or leader. To help firms "get it right" and properly embrace the EOS model, Wickman defined six core areas of focus, including Vision. Entrepreneurs are encouraged to clearly articulate their "three uniques," which define how their business uniquely delivers value to customers. To get this right, they need to know *who* will resonate the most with those unique value propositions.

We also need to ensure we have the right people in the right seats. This may be one of the most overlooked requirements needed to drive success for any sales, marketing, or business endeavor. EOS dictates first determining an organization's core values. Then, using a People Analyzer to determine if individuals embrace the core values, as well as a term called GWC to validate if they're in the right roles. GWC stands for "get it, want it, and have the capacity for it." This might be equated to intuition, inclination, and intellect. EOS also stresses the importance of using data to make sound decisions. To better understand who they currently have on the bus and who should fill the empty seats, many firms use personality tests or profiling assessments. However, most of these were invented twenty to eighty years ago, and almost none leverage the latest neuroscience or visual elements that are more appealing. Most importantly, all but one do not discern for trust—perhaps the most important people factor.

The research completed by Simon Sinek for *Start with Why* was argu-ably not extensive and only covered a handful of firms. However, for *The Challenger Sale*, CEB used a sample size of seven hundred individuals across ninety firms. Later, that grew to 6,000 people—mostly sales profes-sionals. Unfortunately, most of this appears to be anecdotal, such as sales managers being asked their opinion about the attributes displayed by their best and worst sales pros. *The Challenger Sale* authors did not actually attend and analyze sales calls with 6,000 people.

The research documented in *Start with Who* is even more extensive than either of the above-mentioned books. Across more than a decade, field data was collected on over 15,000 salespersons, marketers, cus-tomers, recruiters, and leaders across hundreds of firms and more than 50,000 channel partners worldwide. The research consisted of more than just canned surveys, interviews, and observations but also included actual field trials and real-world usage of the personalization, messag-ing, content, tools, tactics, strategies, frameworks, and methodologies. These were designed and implemented for consulting projects and pro-grams on behalf of such global firms as Adobe, Arrow, Avnet, Better Homes and Gardens Real Estate, Booz Allen Hamilton, Brickwork India, Cisco, Cylance (BlackBerry), Dotmod, Enterprise Rent-A-Car, Fortinet, HP, IBM, Imperva, LogMeIn, Malwarebytes, Oracle, SAP, Patrick Financial, Qualys, Talend, Target, T-Mobile, Visa, VMware, Wells Fargo, and many others.

The results have been unprecedented, but the most important question is whether *Start with Who* will work for you or your firm. The authors of *The Challenger Sale* and similar works cannot guaran-tee results, and neither can this book. Only you can determine if any strategy, tactic, or approach is appropriate for your situation. However, everything presented in this book has gone through rigorous field test-ing. Nothing was included that did not previously deliver stellar results across a large enough universe to be statistically valid.

Does this approach replace any other sales, marketing, business, or recruiting frameworks? Or the theories found in *Start with Why*, VisualStories, Pragmatic Marketing, SPIN Selling, Miller Heiman,

Sandler, Value Selling, or *The Challenger Sale*? It can, but it's designed to augment rather than replace. While a few of the companies that embraced these concepts have standardized on a single framework, most have not. Most have a diverse mixture of business, recruiting, sales, and marketing professionals previously trained on a variety of different approaches and methodologies. Trying to force seasoned pros to adopt new approaches can be difficult and costly. Therefore, the following pages do not recommend a "rip and replace" approach but rather a gradual overlay. No hatchets are required to implement the framework outlined in this book. Instead, virtually any organization can use a simple butter knife to gently layer icing atop whatever cake they already have.

In this book, you'll learn why you shouldn't start with WHY.

You should start with WHO.

CHAPTER 4
PERSUASION

*"If every instinct you have is wrong, then
the opposite would have to be right."*
—Jerry Seinfeld

I n the story that opens this book, once Linda understood *who* she
needed to persuade, she used the Persuasion Model to communicate with and challenge John authoritatively rather than by using an
aggressive, forceful, authoritarian approach.

In between wearing fancy bedsheets and throwing wild toga parties, Aristotle developed *The Art of Rhetoric* starting in 367 BC, which

detailed his triangle of persuasive arguments and formed the basis of his Persuasion Model. Today, top speakers and sales and marketing professionals incorporate these principles into their speeches, messaging, or sales approaches to persuade and inspire audiences and prospects.

One corner of Aristotle's triangle, which he called Pathos, is defined as a "pathetic appeal." Although we've all cringed while witnessing green salespeople or recruiters offer pathetic appeals, Aristotle was referring to a different kind of pathetic. From an emotional perspective, Pathos relates to feelings, suffering, pain, or calamity. Linguistic derivatives of pathos include empathy, sympathy, and apathy. The goal of the "persuader," which could be a speaker, leader, marketer, recruiter, or sales pro, is to appeal to heartstrings and create a shared emotional bond or connection while ensuring the audience doesn't bolt out the door.

Many professionals use a rhetorical approach called enumeration, which is strengthened by making an emotional appeal three times in succession while using three related but different examples. This is not the same as chanting a magic spell three times and hoping your customer or candidate will turn into an easily persuaded frog. The speaker or persuader seeks to trigger key audience emotions that can set up subsequent calls to action, which might be to have them take out their wallet or insist on giving you a purchase order.

Aristotle recommended seven positive emotions as compared to their contrasting negative emotions to accomplish this goal:

- Calmness vs. Anger
- Friendship vs. Enmity
- Confidence vs. Fear
- Shamelessness vs. Shame
- Kindness vs. Unkindness
- Pity vs. Indignation
- Emulation vs. Envy

When employed properly and passionately, with the right motives and intent, Aristotle's Pathos has been used effectively to move an audience to feel what the persuader feels, which in turn creates a bond similar to what one might feel for a close friend or loved one. The right emotional appeal can allow a recruiter, salesperson, marketer, or speaker to connect with their audience and lay a solid foundation for a relationship built on trust.

When you step onto the stage, whether in front of a team, a large audience, or a single person, Aristotle notes that you must connect emotionally. Many sales frameworks, albeit without referring to Aristotle, also recommend this initial approach. Sandler calls this "bonding and rapport." *The Challenger Sale* calls this the "warmer," and so on. Once you have connected emotionally with your audience, you then need to build credibility and trust, which Aristotle called Ethos.

Aristotle used three additional terms to define his views about Ethos. You'll want to memorize all these, as there will be a quiz later, and those who fail will be forced to watch six hours of pathetic selling examples.

Phronesis means good sense. Our bedsheet dude says this is communication that is relevant, tasteful, and appeals to the good sense of the audience.

Arête stands for excellence and good moral character. By showing honest vulnerability, authenticity, and a true heart, a speaker, recruiter, marketer, or salesperson allows the audience to experience arête.

Finally, eunoia refers to goodwill. Your audience needs to sense that your intentions are selfless, and your honest goal is to be helpful by informing them about something important, such as a pending calamity or consequence—which will happen, of course, if they buy a competitive solution or take a job at an inferior company.

We'll later see how these three difficult to pronounce words align with typical sales methodologies, but once you understand how they also form a "brain story," the light bulbs will go off.

The third leg of Aristotle's persuasion triangle is Logos. This is where the speaker or persuader can make a logical argument supported by facts, figures, numbers, validation, success stories, evidence, and reason. A baseball bat also works well here, but I digress. There are two types of arguments that ensure the speaker is properly delivering Logos: deductive and inductive. This final corner of the triangle relates to the closing portion of most sales methodologies, but once we understand what part of the brain we're persuading, miracles can happen. Bonuses and promotions can also happen, so let's pay attention.

Deductive reasons, or arguments, are generally based on specific premises, delivered in small steps, that are true. If one small premise is true, then the next, which builds upon the first, must also be true and therefore the logical conclusion must be valid. Socrates also used this approach by effectively gaining agreement for a small truth and then using that as a stepping stone for the next one. For example, you might say to someone (response noted in italics):

Do you agree the sun will come up in the east tomorrow morning?

Yes, of course I do.

And that it will set in the west in the evening?

Yes, absolutely.

And do so again for the next 365 days?

Yes, without question.

And continue for all the years of your life?

Yes, for the rest of my life.

And that someday, for all of us, we will not witness this event once we're gone?

Yes, sadly that is true.

And you have no idea when that day may come, correct?

Yes, I have no idea when that will be.

Therefore, it's important to ensure the family you leave behind is taken care of, yes?

Yes, very important.

Then wouldn't you agree that it's vitally important to have adequate life insurance?

Ah, well, yes, I guess so.

After having said yes seven times to small unarguable truths, it becomes almost impossible for someone to then say no to the final "closing" question. Unless they're a complete moron, in which case they're probably not a good prospect. Note how this approach differs from the age-old rule that one must always ask open-ended questions. This is true for discovery and tension-building questions asked earlier in a conversation, but the above approach can work well in the latter or closing part of a sale.

Inductive reasoning, where the premises are not certain but offer strong evidence to support the truth, can also be used to invoke Logos. One application of this uses reverse psychology to encourage someone to "sell themselves." As an example, paraphrasing the example given earlier during Linda's initial call with John, a savvy salesperson might employ the following conversational example:

"Are you working with anyone to help you solve your issues, John?"

"Yes, Linda, I contacted another vendor and they're researching answers now."

"Did they inform you of the consequences of deploying an inadequate solution that does not offer a whizzle stick umptifrats?"

"No, they didn't."

"That's very concerning, John. Without a whizzle stick umptifrats you could fry your whittle-me-rig. Even so, if you're happy with the other vendor, then you probably would not entertain a second opinion at this point. I hope I've at least been of some help and would be happy to answer any questions you might have in the future."

"Well, I haven't pulled the trigger with them yet, Linda. Tell me more about this whizzle stick umpti-whatever."

In this example, by offering a morsel of information that included strong evidence of truth, Linda used inductive reasoning to pique curiosity and then politely refused to satisfy the interest. She then used reverse psychology by stating that John might not be interested.

Like many ancient Greeks, Aristotle studied how humans act and react and are persuaded through speech and action. He obviously had no idea that, more than 2,000 years later, modern neuroscientists would not only validate his theories but discover why they work from a scientific "brain story" standpoint. He also had no idea that top salespeople would once again wear fancy bedsheets and throw wild toga parties after far exceeding their quotas.

CONCLUSIONS

- Aristotle wore fancy bed sheets and threw wild toga parties.
- He invented the Persuasion Model.
- To persuade others, we must appeal to emotional, instinctual, and logical triggers.

EXAMPLES

Emotional: "Dude, you're going to love the leather seats in this car. They smell like a cow, and the seat warmer will keep your butt warm for hours."

Instinctual: "This car will automatically correct your driving so when you're drunk, you won't drive over a cliff."

Logical: "There's no logical reason why you should buy this car, except that if you get divorced, you can force your ex to make the payments."

CHAPTER 5

NO BRAINER

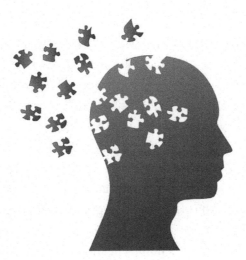

*"The brain is a wonderful organ; it starts work-
ing the moment you get up in the morning and
does not stop until you get into the office."*
—Robert Frost

he late Dr. Paul D. MacLean, a renowned neuroscientist and pretty
cool guy, postulated that humans don't have just one brain, they
have three. I'm pretty sure some people have only half a brain,

like the ones who never give you a purchase order, but again I digress. MacLean shared his theory with the world in his book, *The Triune Brain in Evolution* (MacLean, 1990). He believed that each of our three brains evolved over time and formed three layers, like the layers of a cake, one atop the other. Some are vanilla, some are chocolate, and some are tutti-frutti.

MacLean served as the director of the Laboratory of Brain Evolution and Behavior in Poolesville, Maryland, and commented that our three brains work like three interconnected biological computers with their own intelligence and subjectivity, as well as sense of time, space, and memory.

Some leading neuroscientists agree with MacLean while others do not. For example, Dr. German Garcia-Fresco is the chief science officer for RemotelyMe and the former director of the Adaptive Neuroscience Research Institute in West Hollywood, California. He has a PhD in molecular neurobiology from the University of North Carolina. He and his colleagues (also PhDs) published a paper titled "Neuromarketing: The Science of Selling" (Fresco, 2015) wherein they refer to three brains—rational, emotional, and reptilian. Says Dr. Garcia-Fresco, "I agree that it's not exclusive, but for the most part the human brain can be divided into three areas. The neocortex is more rational, or logical, and involved with reasoning and high-order thinking. The reptilian brain is the oldest part evolutionarily. It is more instinctual and consists of the brain stem and cerebellum. The limbic system or middle brain is where we find the hippocampus and amygdala, which are involved with many of our emotional chemicals and neurotransmitters."

In contrast to Garcia-Fresco and other neuroscientists, Dr. Paul Zak, a neuroeconomics expert with a PhD in economics, disagrees with MacLean and argues that the human brain is a more unified system that is diverse in structure, connection, and function. Those who side with MacLean state that while Zak is correct, it is also true that certain areas of our brain are more involved than others with respect to emotional, instinctual, or logical thought processes and responses.

Says Dr. Garcia-Fresco, "There will always be controversy as the science is still maturing, but I think it is best to align with the science that is the most supported and the least disputed."

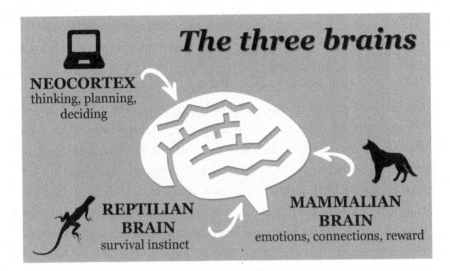

The three brains

NEOCORTEX
thinking, planning, deciding

REPTILIAN BRAIN
survival instinct

MAMMALIAN BRAIN
emotions, connections, reward

The limbic system, or the paleomammalian brain as neurobiologists call it, is comprised of the hippocampus, hypothalamus, and amygdala. Practice saying these five times each and then try it again after five shots of tequila. You'll notice that, with help from your limbic system, you'll become more emotional after downing the tequila. Again, some experts disagree that this part of our brain is "more emotional," but leading neuroscientists say the amygdala is a critical center for coordinating behavioral, autonomic, and endocrine responses to environmental stimuli, especially those with emotional content (Edwards, 2005).

This area of the human mind is involved with love, excitement, heart rate, blood pressure, sweat glands, appetite, sexual desires, and the desire to seek pleasure and avoid pain. It's the part of our brain that keeps us on a barstool well after closing. The limbic system influences someone's attention span, imprints emotionally charged memories, and determines valence—whether a person feels positive, negative, or neutral about something. If you're negative about your mean boss, your limbic system is to blame. Also, it influences salience—whether something or someone captures our attention, like an exciting and sweaty WWE wrestling match. Or a cheesy Hallmark Christmas romance movie. The middle brain also influences value judgments, action rationalizations, and decisions about whether an idea or value proposition is good or bad—the latter being the case if those value props came from a marketing guru. Just kidding.

Areas in the limbic system are stimulated by mild electrical currents that invoke a myriad of emotions, including love, which is influenced by a neuropeptide hormone called oxytocin, produced in the hypothalamus. For women, oxytocin is released during labor and breastfeeding and during sex with a mate. For men, it's also released during sex, but far more so when there is a close bond, such as in a loving relationship. One study (Hurlemann, 2010) published in the *Journal of Neuroscience* noted that oxytocin levels are higher in lovers as compared to single individuals and remain highest during the first six months of a relationship.

Many scientists refer to oxytocin as the "love hormone" (MacGill, 2017) or the "trust hormone" due to its effects on human behavior, most especially its role in love and trust. Oxytocin is responsible for an emotional (loving and trusting) response. Increasing the production of oxytocin also decreases cortisol levels. This hormone controls our instinctual fight or flight responses, which on a short-term basis can save a life by allowing someone to respond quickly to a perilous situation, like losing a sale. Long term, however, cortisol production can be detrimental to your health. Here's an important reminder: over 90 percent of customers buy on trust. If they trust you, your firm, and your solutions, they will buy. If not, they won't. Therefore, if we can increase oxytocin in a customer's brain, they will love us and our brand almost as much they love their dog, and they will trust us enough to give us a big, fat order. The same holds true for recruiters chasing candidates. We'll learn more about how this works in a later chapter.

Dopamine is a neurotransmitter involved with memory, pain/pleasure responses, behavior, cognition, learning, moods, and more (Zak, 2017). It's also released during pleasurable situations, such as the anticipation of or indulgence in something exciting, interesting, and fun—like having sex, eating a juicy hamburger, going on vacation, winning a contest, or closing a deal.

Dopamine and oxytocin predominately affect the limbic system, which is why scientists who side with MacLean believe the limbic system is more involved with emotional responses than other areas (MacLean, 1990). They also note that this part of the brain does not respond well to a communication style or messaging that is logical, including the use of facts, figures, written copy, graphs, and charts.

Pictures, video, audio, tactile, or olfactory (smell) stimuli are usually more effective at eliciting an emotional response. Given this fact, to impact customers or candidates emotionally, sales, marketing, and recruiting professionals should limit the use of spreadsheets and logical value propositions and instead use more pictures, sounds, and vocal timbre. When should you use these? Patience, grasshopper. We'll find out when…and how…in a later chapter.

According to MacLean and other neuroscientists, instinctual areas of the brain include the stem and cerebellum and are responsible for safety responses, harm avoidance, motor balance, and survival instincts. Also, involuntary actions such as heart rate and food digestion. The vagus nerve (Zak, 2017) originates from the brain stem, which is located in the reptilian brain or R-complex (MacLean, 1990). Also, the vagus nerve is where the cortisol "antagonist" bad dude resides.

In Dr. Zak's book *Trust Factor: The Science of Creating High-Performance Companies* (Zak, 2017, p. 300), he states that "trust begets oxytocin" and "high levels of [chronic] stress inhibit the release of oxytocin." While this chemical obviously belongs in the emotional area, it is also the antidote to cortisol-triggered instinctual fight or flight responses.

In an interview, Dr. Zak says, "Think of trust as the biological basis for the Golden Rule: if you treat me nice, my brain makes oxytocin, signaling that you are a person whom I want to be around, so I treat you nice in return."

Some refer to this as the "law of reciprocity," which is usually more effective when not used to manipulate but rather when we sincerely give someone something without expecting the reciprocating gesture. In other words, tit for tat is not nearly as effective as tit for not.

The fear of pain is also an instinctual trigger. Norepinephrine is produced by the adrenal medulla, which is located in an adrenal gland atop the kidneys. Maybe that's why some people pee their pants when terrified. Norepinephrine (noradrenaline) is released by the kidneys, but it affects a part of the brain called the locus coeruleus, which is located in the R-complex brain stem.

MacLean postulated that the reptilian brain (R-complex) is the only part that most reptiles have (MacLean, 1990). A snake, therefore, only acts out of instinctual self-preservation. Maybe that's why some lawyers are called snakes. Just kidding again.

Experts call this brain area the primitive or "basal brain." The instinctual brain is involved in obsessive/compulsive, ritualistic, paranoid, and rigid behaviors, like refusing to reply to your email. It's crammed full of ancestral memories and instincts and drives a person to repeat safe behaviors to ensure longevity. Don't eat that deadly yellow snow, dude.

The instinctual brain is always alert and never sleeps, which is why someone can be instantly awakened by a potential threat. It's motivated by fear of loss, harm, or conflict and is involved with aggression, dominance, and repetition. Mean bosses, obviously, have dominant instinctual brains. We are three times more motivated to avoid harm, loss, or pain than to "gain a gain." If you're a marketer, what's that say about the overuse of value propositions?

Like the limbic system, the instinctual brain does not respond well to written words, numbers, statistics, or logic. It prefers sights, sounds, smells, and touch. Sales and marketing pros who wish to motivate customers to instinctually take action are best not to do so with a presentation or white paper filled with numbers and graphs. Instead, try a Homer Simpson cartoon about potentially losing a chocolate bar.

Gerald Zaltman, a prominent neuroscientist from Harvard University, is the author or editor of over twenty books on various topics involving neuroscience. He stated that at least 90 percent of human cognition is subconscious, while high-order consciousness is only involved with about 10 percent of decision-making (Mahoney, 2003). Dr. Zak agrees with Zaltman that more than 90 percent of decisions are ultimately made by the subconscious mind, which is usually not very logical. We smell the new car leather and all the logic about affording the payments goes out the door. For sales and marketing professionals, when trying to convince someone to make a decision, the use of video is therefore far more effective than a white paper.

There's also a lesson here for recruiters. Nearly all personality or profiling assessments use text-based questions. They're asking someone to make decisions about who they are by appealing to less than 10 percent of their decision-making brain. In contrast, visual stories (pictures, video, audio delivered in a storytelling format) appeal to seven areas across all three "brains" responsible for 100 percent of decision-making. If a picture is worth a thousand words, a video story is worth a million.

In summary, the "instinctual brain" governs norepinephrine, an adrenaline neurotransmitter involved in fight or flight responses. This part of our brain controls cortisol, which is the antithesis to oxytocin. Oxytocin release can foster more trusting and motivated customers or candidates (Zak, 2017, p. 300). The neocortex is the area of the brain that experts like Dr. Zak call the cerebrum, cortex, neopallium, superior, or rational brain (Zak, 2017). These names won't be on the quiz because they take too long to type. The neocortex takes up two-thirds of a human's total brain mass. In animals, it's just the opposite. With some mammals, the neocortex is much smaller and has far fewer folds, which is indicative of less development and complexity. Remove the neocortex from a rat and it will act like a rat. Remove the neocortex from a man and he'll act like a vegetable. He'll also act that way after a pint of vodka.

The cortex is divided into two parts. Although most scientists agree there is no such thing as "right brain versus left brain," it's believed this notion came from the fact that the left cortex controls the right side of the brain and vice versa. An article on ScienceDaily states that the neocortex is involved with the higher functions of the brain, including spatial reasoning, sensory perception, conscious thought, the generation of motor commands, and language processing (ScienceDaily, 2017).

Unlike the other two parts of our brain, persuading or selling someone from a logical perspective is best achieved by using facts, figures, written words, research, graphs, and so on that will appeal more to the neocortex. Pictures, video, and audio can help reinforce concepts, but they will be more effective at stirring emotions and instincts than gaining rational agreement. However, this part of our brain is only responsible for 10 percent of our decision-making. To persuade someone to make a decision, we're best to use more visual and auditory elements, such as video. When added to text, they will appeal to 100 percent of our decision-making brain areas.

As we've learned, well at least most of us, Aristotle believed that to persuade we must appeal to a person's emotional, instinctual, *and* logical "brains." Many neuroscientists concur that the primary chemicals, hormones, and functions that trigger responses are created in or mostly affected by three parts of our brains: the emotional limbic system, the instinctual R-complex, and the logical neocortex. Let's find out how really smart people have used this knowledge to convince people to buy worthless plots of land in Florida.

NEUROMARKETING FOR DUMMIES

Dr. Zaltman patented some of his science under the term Zaltman metaphor elicitation technique (ZMET). By employing ZMET, he explored unconscious behavior using emotional response testing and metaphors to stimulate purchase scenarios. The objective was to create foundational advertising elements, such as images for commercials. This work, combined with other discoveries made by Harvard researchers, led to a new field called neuromarketing, a term coined in 2002 by researcher Ale Smidts (Ariely, 2010).

The use of neuromarketing has expanded rapidly at Apple, Yahoo, eBay, CBS, Google, HP, PepsiCo, Ford Motor Co., Hyundai, Hewlett-Packard, Frito-Lay, Coca-Cola, Procter & Gamble, and many other companies worldwide. For example, one firm experimented with an ad showing a baby sitting next to the headline. By simply turning the baby's head to look at the headline, they doubled eye focus and attention. Yahoo learned that by changing one color on a call-to-action button, they could increase click-through rates by over 30 percent.

Various techniques brought to the party by neuromarketing have made significant differences in audience reactions, and three elements often employed by neuromarketers include the use of contrasts, colors, and the power of three.

CONTRASTS

Think of a typical storytelling arc. In the beginning of the story, on the left side of a page, the protagonist begins her journey in a flawed, unfulfilled, and unhappy state. She travels through the middle of this story and winds up on the opposite side of the page at the end of the story as wise, happy, and less flawed. This is an example of contrast. In like manner, we're best to have a "where you are" picture on the left side or top of a page and a "where you could be" pic on the right side or (scroll down) bottom. "See, Mr. Prospect, by allowing us to help you through your Buyer's Journey, you can go from schmuck to luck just like this guy."

COLORS

In workshops, I dive into this topic in great detail. For now, recall the high school physics acronym Roy G. Biv. It's all about wavelengths. The dark red wavelength is 700 nanometers, and brighter red is 665. As this decreases, we transition through orange, yellow, green, blue, indigo, and then violet. This spells Roy G. Biv.

Neuron Color Spectrum

Wavelength	Positive Emotion	Neuron Stimulation	Negative Emotion	Neuron Stimulation
Red 630 - 780 nm	Passion, Importance, Energy, Excitement	Dopamine Norepinephrine	Anger, Fear, Impact, Aggression	Cortisol Norepinephrine
Orange 590 - 630 nm	Playful, Energetic, Fun, Frugal	Dopamine Norepinephrine	Concern, Ignorance, Deceit, Edgy	Cortisol Norepinephrine
Yellow 570 - 590 nm	Happy, Friendly, Easy, Simple	Dopamine Norepinephrine	Caution, Criticism, Jealousy, Lazy	Cortisol
Green 500 - 570 nm	Natural, Safe, Stable, Harmonious	Serotonin Oxytocin	Money, Greed, Mistrust, Jealousy	Cortisol
Blue 450 - 500 nm	Serene, Trustworthy, Inviting, Calm	GABA Oxytocin	Tired, Uninterested, Dispassionate	Cortisol Serotonin
Indigo 420 - 500 nm	Dependable, Expert, Peaceful	GABA Serotonin	Depressed, Cold, Passive	GABA Serotonin
Violet 390 - 420 nm	Luxurious, Mysterious	GABA	Gloomy, Sad, Moody	GABA

As we can see from this chart, various colors impact our brains in different ways. There's a reason why insane asylums use blue paint on their walls. Crazy people like blue, which happens to be my favorite color. No comments, please. More accurately, blue's color spectrum has a more calming effect on the brain, whereas red is more alarming—which is why it's used in traffic lights to signal stop. Our emotional brain responds better to lighter yellow, green, or blue colors, our instinctual brain to red, orange, or black. Our logical brain is a bit crazy and likes lower wavelengths like darker blue, indigo, and violet.

In short, higher wavelengths trigger more instinctual R-complex activity. Medium wavelengths stimulate more limbic emotional responses, and lower wavelengths more neocortex calming and logical reactions.

THE POWER OF THREE

We've all seen PowerPoint slides with a million bullets and words and rolled our eyes. After squinting for an hour, does the presenter really expect us to remember all these facts? Perhaps because our triune brains are divided into three parts, we're wired to prefer information delivered in threes. On the count of three. Ready, set, go. Three strikes you're out. When delivering information in any form, we're best to focus on only three things at once. Our PowerPoint slides should have only three short bullets, not the Encyclopedia Britannica.

As noted in the title and mentioned earlier, once we know *who* we're trying to persuade, we should strive to convey almost any concept with four pictures, twelve bullet points, and a story about *why* someone should care. We'll later explore how to use one picture or graphic and three bullets for each act in the 3-Act Sales Play to deliver powerful stories to customers or candidates that will have them quivering with excitement. No, really.

While neuroscientists and neuromarketers would like to believe their discoveries and concepts are groundbreaking, Aristotle obviously had a glimpse of this concept when he created his Persuasion Model eons ago. Also, George Ivanovich Gurdjieff, a Russian philosopher and teacher (of Greek descent), often referred to humans as "three-brained beings" (Howell, 2012). One brain for the body (gut), one for the spirit (head), and one for the soul (heart). Plato referred to similar concepts, as did Kabbalah spiritual leaders.

Credible Visual Contrasts

VS.

The Power of 3

3 Act Play
3 Characters
3 Choices

Given that talent acquisition, sales, marketing, and business professionals are trying to persuade and sell to *people* and not accounts, territories, or personas, it stands to reason that an understanding of modern neuroscience and the triune brain as it relates to motivating people can help us refrain from having to twist arms to get a sale, recruit someone, or lead a team.

Next up is a chapter that will literally blow your mind.

CONCLUSIONS

- We have three brains, but fortunately, we don't have three eyes because that would look weird.
- Our three brains are more emotional, instinctual, or logical. Sound familiar? If not, dress up in a fancy bedsheet.
- Our emotional brain prefers more visual, auditory, or tactile stimulation and medium wavelength colors (yellow and green). Our instinctual brain also prefers pictures and videos and higher wavelength colors (red and orange). Our logical brain likes words and numbers and lower wavelength colors (blue and violet).

Our brains also retain and respond better to information delivered using contrasts and in groups of three. Ready, set, let's go to the next chapter.

CHAPTER 6

PSYCHO BABBLE

"If you think you can do a thing or think
you can't do a thing, you're right."
—Henry Ford

Most psychologists are dying to know who you are. The term "psychology" is derived from the Greek words psyche, meaning "spirit, soul, and breath," and logia, which means "the study of something." Psychology is the study of mental and behavioral processes, or how humans interact with and react to the world around them. In other words, *who* they are. Psychology is also the study of the small-minded, which may be why psychologists are also called shrinks.

Ancient Greek philosophers were the founders of psychology, but the German psychologist Wilhelm Wundt set up the first "psych lab" back in 1879 (Kleinman, 2012a, p. 7). Since then, the science has spurred dozens of studies and theories about what makes people "tick." It's also helped furniture manufacturers sell lots of leather couches.

One of the most well-known psychologists in history is Sigmund Freud (Kleinman, 2012b, pp. 20–31). Born in 1865, Freud spent most of his life in Vienna, where he wrote three books about dream interpretation, psychopathology, and sexuality. He also had a lot of fun researching his concepts. To no surprise, Freud is remembered most for his sex studies, but he also gave the world many of its modern concepts about the human id, ego, and superego. Like Dr. MacLean, Freud observed that humans have three brains, but lacking neuroscientific knowledge, he did not understand why.

The id refers to that unorganized portion of the personality structure related to basic animal instincts and bodily needs. The id is motivated by pain and pleasure. Naturally, people want to avoid one and seek the other. As babies, all humans are controlled almost entirely by the id, which is why some kids whine every time they get hungry. Some adults still do that; you know who you are.

As we become adults, we learn to control id impulses lest we pee in our pants or attack a waiter at a fancy restaurant with a fork rather than wait patiently to be served. Addictions and severe temper tantrums stem from an inability to properly control id impulses. The id is the raw animal within everyone, the untamed beast, unconcerned with right, wrong, good, evil, or morality. Within the id resides the instinctual drive to survive. Also, the desire to drive really fast.

Superego is the learned stuff. Rules, guidelines, boundaries, etiquette, proper communication skills, flushing the toilet, saying thank you, etc., all reside in the superego domain. Most learned these appropriate behaviors from parents, teachers, siblings, friends, and so forth.

When someone did something bad, they were given pain, such as a belt whipping from Dad. When they did something good, they received a dose of pleasure, like ice cream from Mom. The superego learned how to behave appropriately through this process of emotional pain and pleasure learning.

The ego deals with the part of personality structure that controls the perceptive, defensive, cognitive, and executive functions. Reason and common sense stem from the ego. A primary ego function is to mitigate between the id and superego while striking the right balance between primitive drive and modern reality. The ego logically organizes thoughts and makes sense of them. Unlike the id, wherein raw passions reside, the ego deals with reason and common sense. When the ego is healthy, people have better control over base instincts, such as the need to lash out in anger or run from potential conflict.

Freud's conclusions intimate that the id is predominately involved with instinctual brain functions. The superego appears to be more involved with emotional functions, and the ego is rational and pragmatic and more logical. Could it be that Freud had the same observations as the ancient Greeks? It appears that both proffered the concept of humans having three distinct brains that tend to be more emotional, instinctual, or logical. Maybe Freud should have worn bedsheets.

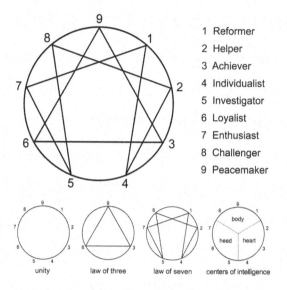

1 Reformer
2 Helper
3 Achiever
4 Individualist
5 Investigator
6 Loyalist
7 Enthusiast
8 Challenger
9 Peacemaker

The enneagram symbol is an interconnected circle made of nine points used to depict nine distinct personality types. Some people believe the ancient Greeks invented the diagram and science, and evidence of its origination can be found in 4,000-year-old Pythagorean geometry. The Pythagoreans were an inquisitive bunch and were captivated by the deeper meaning and significance of numbers. They also liked wine. Plato apparently studied the enneagram theories and passed them on to his disciple Plotinus and other followers.

George Gurdjieff, a Russian teacher and follower of Freud, learned about the enneagram in the 1920s while visiting a Sufi monastery in Afghanistan (Howell, 2012). Oscar Ichazo learned about it from Gurdjieff, and Claudio Naranjo heard about it from Ichazo. Basically, he heard it from a friend who heard it from a friend. He probably wrote a song about it. Robert Ochs and Helen Palmer researched the enneagram by studying Naranjo's concepts, but the most famous authors on the enneagram are Don Richard Riso and Russ Hudson of the Enneagram Institute.

Some question whether the enneagram is accurate. The ancient Greeks invented the water mill, odometer, alarm clock, cartography, geometry, medicine, philosophy, and democracy. They excelled in the fields of astronomy, biology, and physics. Aristotle postulated that our world was round, and the Pythagoreans proposed that the earth revolved around the sun, which is why they liked wine. Archimedes discovered that submerging a solid object displaces a like measure of weight. The Greeks weren't infallible, but lacking the distraction of Netflix, they were highly observant and spent hours watching the stars and each other. It is possible the research conducted by the Greeks on human personalities is bunk, but considering the advanced knowledge displayed by the ancients who used the enneagram, this appears to be unlikely. Moreover, given recent discoveries made by modern neuroscientists, it also seems that the personality profiles outlined in the enneagram are quite accurate.

***

During the early 1900s, humanist psychologist Carl Rogers proffered his "self-theory" (Kleinman, 2012c, pp. 115–118). He believed all humans are infused with a single driving motivation: to self-actualize. He defined this state as achieving the highest level of "human-being-ness." He obviously never watched a hockey game. Others have simplified this theory to being happy or filled with joy in every aspect of one's life—including professions.

Modern psychology views personality through the lens of an individual's emotions, behaviors, thoughts, actions, and reactions. These make people unique in relation to others and are referred to as mental models (Johnson-Laird, 2012, pp. 131–138). Although humans exhibit personality characteristics in individualized ways, there are definite commonalities. Traits remain relatively constant throughout someone's entire life. The caveat here is whether they are acting in healthy or unhealthy ways.

In addition, individual or not, people tend to behave in similar and sometimes predictable ways when faced with certain situations or decisions. Most of us will run away from the abominable snowman. Although the study of personality is decidedly a psychological science, many experts now agree that personalities are impacted by neurological wiring and processes. Some psychologists, like Sigmund Freud, subscribe to the "nature" theory, in which they believe biology (today more commonly referred to as neuropsychology) entirely governs our personalities (Kleinman, 2012c). Others, like Alfred Adler, lean toward the "nurture" theory in which personalities are governed entirely by experiences, environment, and societal factors (Kleinman, 2012d). For Freud and other nature theorists, Homer Simpson was born an idiot and his mother had little to do with it. For Alfred and the nurturists (not a rock band), Homer's mom is entirely to blame.

Many other experts have a leg in both camps. They point to identical twins or triplets exposed to similar environments and home situations who exhibit completely different personalities. They claim nature is to blame for core personality types, but different nurturing aspects can alter levels of psychological health and account for diverse individuality.

In the mid-1930s, Gordon Allport, a Harvard graduate, became the first psychologist in the United States to teach a class about personalities (Kleinman, 2012e). He also created a trait theory using more than 4,500 dictionary words to describe different traits. He divided these traits into three categories he named cardinal (individual), central (common), and secondary (conditional) traits. Years later, Raymond Cattell reduced Allport's long list down to 171 traits by combining and reclassifying similarities and removing uncommon ones. Using questionnaires completed by individual subjects, he narrowed the list even further to only sixteen types that include perfectionism, dominance, apprehension, and warmth. Allport's observations provided some of the foundational elements used in the sixteen Myers-Briggs personality profiles.

OPQ32 is a personality "test" widely used in professional and employment circles for selection, development, team building, succession planning, and organizational change. The SHL Group, purveyors of the OPQ, completed a study in 2005 in concert with the Enneagram Institute and discovered that the nine personality types proliferated by the ancients are real and objective and stand on a par with Myers-Briggs, the Big Five, and other prominent psychological systems (Brown & Bartram, 2005).

The OPQ32, backed by hundreds of validation studies across tens of thousands of individuals, is one of the most widely used and highly regarded measures of personality in the workplace. Professors Dave Bartram and Anna Brown conducted an independent study of the Enneagram Institute interpretation made by authors Don Riso and Russ Hudson to see if it related to the OPQ32 and discovered a clear match.

Bartram and Brown reviewed information from hundreds of volunteer participants from different countries. The results indicated a strong relationship between the nine enneagram personality types and OPQ32 traits. In fact, based on a person's OPQ32 profile, someone could predict the enneagram type 75 percent of the time. One could do this only 11 percent of the time by guessing. Unless, of course, they're psychic, which is not one of the personality types.

There are dozens of personality tests similar to OPQ32, Myers-Briggs, and the rest, as well as job performance tests used by recruiters. So what's the problem with all these tests? They use words. We learned earlier that our logical brain is responsible for less than 10 percent of our decision-making. Also, that part of our brain responds best to text, words, numbers, etc. Our emotional and instinctual brains, responsible for 90 percent of our decision-making, respond best to visual, auditory, or tactile information. Therefore, as they only access the logical brain, tests invented decades ago that use text or words are often 50 to 75 percent valid as based on Cronbach's Alpha test validation techniques. Studies show that just 30 percent of individuals complete these tests, which often consist of fifty to a hundred questions and take thirty to ninety minutes to complete.

What's needed is a new approach that uses visual neuroscience storytelling to appeal to 100 percent of the decision-making brain, not just 10 percent. An assessment that predominately uses video elements that appeal to all three of our brains. One that has a 97 percent completion rate and almost 93 percent Cronbach's Alpha validity. Fortunately, this groundbreaking new approach to talent assessments for recruiting and prospect assessments is now available. It's a new approach called Visual Neuroscience Assessment™. Dr. German Garcia-Fresco, the neuroscientist referred to earlier, along with Dr. Aaron Aronow, a renowned neurosurgeon at the University of Southern California (USC), conducted field trials to determine if—and how—specific brain chemical and neurotransmitter levels relate to personality traits. Subjects first completed a CQ assessment, which is a test designed to determine one of nine distinct personality tendencies, as well as introversion versus extroversion, for a total of eighteen. The results offer a few similarities to the enneagram and Myers-Briggs Type Indicator but far surpass these and all others by providing indications related to the levels of norepinephrine, serotonin, oxytocin, GABA, dopamine, and acetylcholine.

This new viewpoint could potentially pull the rug out from under *The Challenger Sale* conclusions. Neuroscience now tells us that there are not five types of salespersons but instead nine types corresponding to different brain profiles. In the next chapter, we'll see how our brain biology determines how logical, emotional, or instinctual we are, as well as our degrees of extroversion or introversion. Understanding this can help sales, marketing, business, and recruiting professionals unlock the door to a prospect or candidate's head, heart, and gut to motivate them to take action.

A FEW MORE THOUGHTS

Virtually all personality profiling models seek to determine who we are and have been based upon observational science dating back thousands of years, beginning with the creation of the ancient enneagram model. This science was not updated until a few hundred years ago when psychologists developed early personality profiling models, again based on observations.

More recently, respected institutions and researchers have expanded upon or streamlined historical personality profiling models to create frameworks and systems used for professional environments such as employment screening and jury selection. Also, for dating and ridiculing your friends. However, all these models still rely on observational science—what has been observed across thousands of individuals—to create profiles that appear to be only "ballpark" correct. More importantly, nearly all these assessments use text-based questions, which only appeal to our logical brain—responsible for only 10 percent of decision-making. Modern neuroscience and research conducted by experts in this new field offer validation in some respects for these older models while providing the opportunity to create more effective and useful frameworks for sales, marketing, recruiting, and other fields. A new approach called CareerQuotient (CQ) uses this new Visual Neuroscience storytelling approach to access the entire brain, responsible for 100 percent of decision-making. This new type of assessment also offers 25 to 45 percent more accuracy and three times the completion rate in less than one-fourth the time on average.

Neuroscientific research also now calls into question the conclusions drawn by the authors of *The Challenger Sale*, which are based solely on observational opinions. Given nine personality types, it may be invalid to state that a particular type of salesperson is more effective than another, based on a quantitative measurement of observed sales success. After all, success for most firms is not always measured by near-term closed sales and has in recent years become far more of a "team sport." Is a short running back better than a taller one? If a running back does not score on every drive, is he a bad football player or is his offensive line subpar?

As we'll observe in the next chapter, it's not realistic to expect that a Relationship Builder salesperson can simply shed his or her skin and miraculously become a Challenger salesperson any more than a zebra can become a lion. More importantly, how do you define a Relationship Builder as compared to a Challenger? Do we really believe that a salesperson who seeks to build a relationship with a customer is doomed to fail?

Last but not least, could the reason *why* some individuals fail is because of *who* they are?

CONCLUSIONS

- We're all insane, but it's not our fault. We're all wired that way.
- Sigmund Freud, when he wasn't screwing around, also determined that we have three brains and we're all insane.
- There's a new profile assessment approach, called Visual Neuroscience, that uses neuroscience storytelling to validate that we're all insane.

CHAPTER 7

NOT SO CHALLENGING

"The only place success comes before
work is in the dictionary."
—Vince Lombardi

The number one finding in *The Challenger Sale* is that there are five types of sales reps. This finding was derived from hundreds of surveys completed by "frontline sales managers across ninety companies around the world." In other words, they relied primarily on the definitions and descriptions provided from surveys rather than frontline observations across thousands of actual sales calls or meetings with customers.

More recent field and scientific studies now indicate that the definitions used for the five salesperson types in *The Challenger Sale* may be questionable. Furthermore, neuroscience intimates there are nine types and not five because studies validate nine types of *people*. This scientific conclusion has been further supported by thousands of documented, and in many cases recorded, sales calls and meetings that spanned a decade across dozens of industries.

For finding #1, *The Challenger Sale* defined the five types as:

1. The Relationship Builder (21 percent of sample, 7 percent of high performers)

- Classic consultative selling approach
- Seeks to find internal sponsors
- Fosters strong relationships with prospects

Relationship Builders focus on developing personal and professional relationships throughout an account. These reps are generous with their knowledge and time and seek to meet customer needs. They strive to resolve any tensions that arise and maintain a strong relationship. The authors intimated that while most firms encourage and empower this type of selling, it is the least effective of the five types.

The problem with these conclusions seems obvious. The authors are not describing problems with sales pros but with sales managers and trainers. The Relationship Builders described here are not sales pros, they are customer service agents. These reps were *allowed* to do nothing more than service accounts. This is not a personality "type" issue, it's a hiring, management, and training issue.

2. The Reactive Problem Solver (14 percent of sample, 12 percent of high performers)

- Very detail oriented
- Reliable and responsive to stakeholders
- Seeks to solve all problems

Reactive Problem Solvers are reliable and detail oriented. They focus on post-sales follow-up to ensure that any service issues are addressed and resolved quickly and effectively. Many of us who have managed sales teams have seen this type of person break sales records. Again, this is not a "type" problem but a management issue. If we divide 100 percent by five types, we get 20 percent, and the sample size is only 14 percent. As such, 12 percent can become 20 percent with proper management, support, and training.

3. The Hard Worker (21 percent of sample, 17 percent of high performers)

- Doesn't give up easily
- Self-motivated
- Interested in feedback and personal development

Hard Workers show up early, stay late, and always go the extra mile. These reps are hard drivers and can make more calls in an hour and meet with more prospects in a week than other types. Why is this a problem? Most sales managers would give a bottle of Macallan 18 for a Hard Worker. Again, 17 percent out of a possible 20 percent ain't bad. Also, are the authors saying that none of the other types are hard workers? How did they segregate this type from the rest? Is everyone else lazy?

4. The Lone Wolf (18 percent of sample, 25 percent of high performers)

- Instinctual, does not follow rules
- Self-assured and self-confident
- Delivers results; difficult to manage

Lone Wolves are self-confident and have the natural ability to succeed based on instincts. They break the rules, are hard to manage, and do things their own way. They are the least common profile but are the second most common type among top performers. I've not met a single sales exec who hasn't managed this type of person. Yeah, they're a challenge (every pun intended), but obviously they get the job done. Again, give me a team of Lone Wolves that are 25 percent of my top performers and I'm all in. Also again, are they saying that none of the other types are Lone Wolves? Everyone else is an angelic team player?

5. The Challenger (27 percent of sample, 39 percent of high performers)

- Adopts a different world view
- Enjoys debates and challenging customer beliefs
- Deep understanding of their customers' business

Challengers research and understand their customers' business and challenge their thinking and belief systems. They seek to maintain control of the sales conversation and are not afraid to express controversial views. They have a strong, assertive, and controlling communication style. They are the most common type among top performers. This seems more like a polished, disciplined, well-trained, and supported sales pro rather than a "type" of person. In other words, if you scan hundreds of résumés, you likely won't find a Challenger.

You may find a top performer, but they might also be a Lone Wolf. Even so, they probably played for a great team. Let's be honest, Tom Brady has far fewer Super Bowl rings if he's on teams with bad coaches and lousy defenses. Sure, he gets all or most of the credit, but it's impossible to throw a touchdown pass without a receiver.

Based on this research, the authors concluded that:

- 39 percent of top sales performers used a Challenger-style approach
- Top performers were more than twice as likely to use a Challenger approach
- Over half of top performers fit the Challenger profile for complex sales
- Only 7 percent of top performers used the Relationship Building approach
- Across core or average performers, all five types were essentially equal performers

The authors stated that "mediocrity comes in multiple flavors." This is the most profound statement in the book and undermines the authors' conclusions about "types" of salespersons or the approach they use. If you have an average salesperson, it does not matter which approach is employed, they are still average. Virtually every firm I've engaged with, and every sales exec I've conversed with, have come to the same conclusions: top performers can always benefit from adjustments, but if we can turn our "average hitters" into "silver sluggers," we'll always exceed quotas. The question is, how do we do that without breaking the bank... or our backs?

This theory holds true for recruiters as well. After all, at the end of the day, recruiters are also essentially salespersons. They're tasked with finding prospects (candidates), understanding how to qualify and motivate them, and finally, close them on joining their firm. In short, they sell.

More recent research shows that rather than use a single sales approach, as assumed by the authors of *The Challenger Sale*, top sales performers use a variety of approaches that optimally align with their personality profiles and are situationally based on the circumstances and buyer type—in the same way top leaders use the situational leadership style created by Ken Blanchard, co-author of *The New One Minute Manager*.

To state that a Challenger salesperson (based on their approach and sales methodology) is more successful than a Relationship Builder, for example, because statistically more of them are top performers may be as questionable as concluding that because there are more male CEOs in business, women lack the ability to succeed. Virtually any woman, after smacking you in the face, will quickly debunk this obviously incorrect conclusion.

Let's dig deeper into the research about each of *The Challenger Sale* types to find out why the definitions may be inaccurate.

RELATIONSHIP BUILDERS

By the definition used in *The Challenger Sale*, a Relationship Builder is generous with time, strives to meet every need, and resolve tensions. They also "get along with everyone." This sounds more like a friendly customer service rep than a sales pro. The disconnect here may be in the definition used by the authors. During research conducted for this book, when top sales professionals were asked for their definition of relationship building, all gave vastly different perspectives than the one used in *The Challenger Sale*. Across virtually any industry, top performers all stated that the key to their success was building relationships, but they never defined it as being generous with time, getting along with everyone, resolving tensions, or creating harmony. Instead, they saw it as fostering friendships and trust built upon integrity, honesty, and reliability. They sought to use collaboration, understanding, empathy, and caring to deliver high value. These qualities do not seem to align with the ones described by *The Challenger Sale* for any of the five types.

The conclusion here is that based on the definition used by *The Challenger Sale* authors, this type of sales rep was set up for failure and had no chance to succeed. It's like saying that a four-foot-nine high schooler will be the worst performer on a professional basketball team. Well, duh.

REACTIVE PROBLEM SOLVERS

The Challenger Sale describes these reps as such: "They come into the office in the morning with grand plans to generate new sales, but as soon as an existing customer calls with a problem, they dive right in rather than passing it to the people we actually pay to solve those problems."

Having directed several inside sales teams, and having been involved with the training of thousands of reps across dozens of clients worldwide, I've never met a sales manager that tolerated this kind of behavior for more than a month, let alone a quarter. This is likely not a good sales rep but could perchance be a great customer service rep.

Again, the definition used in *The Challenger Sale* describes a possible behavioral or hiring issue rather than a sales approach and leaves no room for rep success. This type is like a five-foot-four basketball player on the court next to Stephen Curry.

HARD WORKERS

Years ago, as a sales director, I had two completely different individuals on my team. One was extroverted, gregarious, and great with customers. They all loved him. He could run circles around a phone conversation and was voted as the most likely sales rep to succeed. Problem was, he was not a hard worker. He showed up late, was not organized, didn't hit the phones consistently, and took long breaks.

The other guy on my team had half the skills and talent, but he had a lot of heart. He was like the football player Rudy at Notre

Dame—five-foot-nothing but gave it his all. He was a hard worker but initially did not have lots of sales success because he lacked the ability. He was voted most likely *not* to succeed. What happened to these two?

I took them both under my wing and did my own hard work to train, coach, and motivate them. The first guy had some initial success, but he later defaulted to being lazy and was eventually fired. The second rep struggled at first but put his head down, came in early and went home late, went the extra mile, and made more calls in a week than anyone else. With some coaching, enablement, and training, he became the best performer in the company and won lots of awards.

The moral of this story? Based solely on the definition used by the authors of *The Challenger Sale*, this type should not be very successful. However, their research does not "go the extra mile" by determining whether these reps *could* be successful if properly trained, coached, and nurtured along the path to success. That does not mean they can only succeed if they become a Challenger type; however, using some of the techniques recommended, such as challenging beliefs, can help anyone become more successful. Again, this is not a salesperson-type issue, it's a training challenge. This person will still be a "hard worker."

As such, they are like a six-foot basketball player who may not score as many points as other players, but with proper coaching they can be an outstanding defensive player, excellent rebounder, and a very valuable member of the team. Championships are won or lost with the help of these kinds of players, but only if their coach recognizes their value and empowers them to succeed.

LONE WOLVES

The authors of *The Challenger Sale* state that Lone Wolves are the rule breakers of the sales force who march to a different beat and do things any way they want. They don't update CRM systems, complete trip reports, or follow sales processes. They create their own content without using templates, thumb their noses at managers, and come in second on the performance meter.

The authors note that "Lone Wolves tend to do very well despite egregiously flouting the system, because if they didn't do well, they'd have been fired already."

By this definition, as a sales manager, I should rejoice if a Lone Wolf shows up at my door looking for a job. Yet every sales manager is constantly frustrated by this type. They are uncontrollable, disrespectful, and impossible to manage. What's the answer? Hire, fire, force, or just hope for the best?

The answer to this question is that this type, and any other type, can't be changed, because they're hardwired by neuroscience. The best way to deal with them is to create reasonable yet flexible boundaries and implement systems and processes that allow them to be who they are while improving their ability to win deals. They are like Draymond Green on the Golden State Warriors basketball team. Invaluable, but prone to anger bouts and lots of technical fouls. As long as the former far outweighs the latter, the team will never trade this guy.

CHALLENGERS

We've all heard the age-old joke that timid salespeople have skinny kids. According to the authors of *The Challenger Sale*, bold individuals are the golden boys and girls who can do no wrong and consistently win more deals than anyone. They will never have skinny kids. However, they recount attributes and characteristics rather than selling styles or methodologies. They are described as debaters, assertive, and strong two-way communicators. Again, these are usually characteristics and not necessarily approaches.

The authors say this "type" seeks to understand a customer's business, take control of a conversation, and challenge them on their beliefs and thinking. They are relatively fearless about debating controversial issues and tend to display thought leadership. They also offer customers unique perspectives and are not afraid to pressure them or discuss pricing and other sensitive topics.

These are seven-footers with great three-point shooting ability that every basketball team wants. Unfortunately, as in sports, these elite individuals are far and few between and usually very expensive. Also, as noted earlier, they are usually supported by an excellent team.

Finding #2 for *The Challenger Sale*, based on the above definitions, is that there is one clear winner and one clear loser. Challengers are winners and Relationship Builders are losers. Seven-foot, three-point dunkers are winners and four-foot-ten high school students are losers on the basketball court. Brilliant observation, Sherlock.

If you're a sales, marketing, or corporate executive, having just read *The Challenger Sale*, you might be inclined to instruct HR to hire only seven-footers. Problem is, every other team wants them as well. You might also consider firing anyone in sales who tries to build a relationship with a customer, as if that's a bad thing. Problem is, another team with a differing viewpoint will hire them and steal all your best customers, because the reps you fired own the relationships.

What about your core or average reps? Should you try to do what *The Challenger Sale* recommends? Spend millions to force all these reps to become Challengers? Force them all to abandon their previous training, be it SPIN, Miller Heiman, Sandler, or whatever, and adopt only the Challenger framework? Force tigers to be lions?

What if there was a less disruptive, more affordable, and more effective approach? What if we could identify nine types of sales professionals by identifying their neuroscience-based profiles? Then, train them to use a simple yet powerful sales approach that did not require a difficult or expensive rip-and-replace? What if you could then use advanced storytelling, just-in-time sales enablement tools, LinkedIn Social Selling, effective sales coaching, and personalized account-based marketing to turn .200 hitters into consistent .300 hitters within a few quarters? As icing on the cake, what if they were also supported by a system that uses ChatGPT to create personalized emails or messages within seconds based on LinkedIn and neuroscience profiles?

What if this new approach complemented and aligned with *The Challenger Sale* and virtually any other sales methodology or framework?

Is this nirvana or just a pipe dream? We'll discover the answer to this question in the next few chapters. We'll also learn that empowering, inspiring, and enabling sales professionals to perform at their best is more about effective leadership and engagement than a sales or marketing methodology. It's also about teaching them how to tell stories that build trust.

CONCLUSIONS

- It may be time to challenge *The Challenger Sale*.
- There are not five types of salespersons, there are nine, and they can all be trained to sell.
- You can't force tigers to be lions, but you can teach both how to roar.

CHAPTER 8

OVER THE RAINBOW

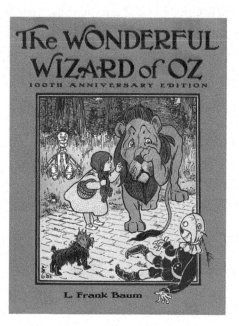

"It is an ancient need to be told stories.
But the story needs a great storyteller."
—Alan Rickman

 efore we can apply storytelling techniques to persuade customers or candidates to take action, we first need to understand *how* to tell a story. Decades ago, as a green writer with stars in my eyes,

I attended a writing workshop in Maui, Hawaii. I walked in the room with an attitude, certain that I was the world's best storyteller. I soon learned how wrong I was. I had no idea how to create a sympathetic character in a Hero's Journey, raise the stakes in an escalating plot, craft engaging dialogue, use misdirection, open and close scenes, leverage active verbs to ensure dynamic pacing, and so on. Humbled but motivated, I listened and practiced. By the end of the workshop, I was voted most improved. I wasn't sure I should feel proud about that achievement or just the opposite, and I realized it might be years before I could truly call myself a storyteller.

Does that mean most sales and marketing pros have little hope of becoming masterful storytellers? Not at all. However, let's be realistic. It's not fair to toss a junior marketer into the fire and expect them to write a bestseller overnight. Also, even if a salesperson or recruiter is a gifted writer, properly applying storytelling techniques in a sales or talent acquisition scenario is not something one learns in a writing class. With training and practice, however, most professionals can eventually run circles around untrained counterparts, who hopefully work for competitors.

Aristotle taught us via his ancient Persuasion Model that to persuade we must expand the way in which we communicate to include logical, emotional, and instinctual appeals. One of the most effective ways to do this is by using compelling and engaging stories because "facts tell and stories sell." We've been telling stories ever since that first caveman speared a bison and lived to tell about it. When told well, stories usually follow the three-act play format often employed in the plays of Shakespeare, the poetry of Aristotle, the fables of Aesop, and movies directed by Alfred Hitchcock. Humans thrive on stories. They engage our minds and help us connect ideas, understand ourselves and others, and learn complex concepts. The lessons learned through stories are far more memorable and often leave a deeper, more impactful, and longer lasting impression on our minds. They speak more directly to our emotional and instinctual brains and have a higher retention factor than logic-based presentations.

The London Business School conducted studies and found that a properly structured story can increase retention by 1400 percent. Dr. Paul Zak tells us why. When tensions and stakes ramp during a story, the chemical cortisol is released, which heightens attention and retention. Facts, figures, and logical value propositions only impact two parts of our logical brain, whereas a good story touches seven parts of our brain across logical, emotional, and instinctual centers.

Storytelling approach

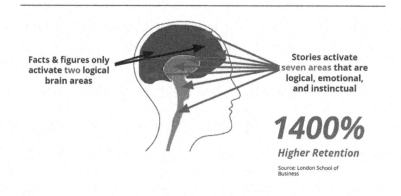

Facts & figures only activate two logical brain areas

Stories activate seven areas that are logical, emotional, and instinctual

1400%
Higher Retention

Source: London School of Business

Neuroscience explains why stories are more engaging and stay with us longer than the factual copy we might read in a textbook or see on a PowerPoint slide. Researchers in Spain, while conducting studies in 2006, discovered that certain words such as "rose" or "mint" were understood by the language-processing area of our brain but also activated networks in the olfactory regions responsible for processing odors. Our brain actually smells a rose when we read a description about the sweet fragrant sent. Don't believe me? Imagine a bright yellow juicy sour lemon. You're biting into the citrus pulp of a bitter lemon right now and the sour juice is flowing across your taste buds. Are you salivating yet? If not, perhaps you're a zombie or a vampire or you've been trained by the CIA to trick lie detector tests.

Words unassociated with our senses, such as "button" or "coat," don't stimulate anything. You're fastening the button on your coat right now. Feel anything? Didn't think so.

Motion words also have an interesting effect on our brain. If we're reading a good thriller, for example, and the author is describing a high-speed chase, certain words will trigger our motor cortex—the part of our brain that controls muscular movement. Researchers used an fMRI system to show that when individuals read the words "kick," "pick," or "lick," brain areas controlling their feet, fingers, or tongue start tapping or licking.

Jeffrey Zacks, the director of the Dynamic Cognition Laboratory at Washington University in St. Louis, said neuroscientists and psychologists are learning how stories can create a mental simulation of described events. Zacks and his team conducted a study in 2009 wherein fMRI scans were used on participants to record various regions of the brain stimulated by short stories. This study revealed that when we become engrossed in fictional events happening to a story character, we feel and react as if they are real. Whether it's real or we're reading about it in a good book, the exact same areas in our brain light up.

This phenomenon is triggered by mirror neurons in our brain. Mirror neurons were discovered in the 1980s by neuroscientist Dr. Giacomo Rizzolatti and his team from the University of Parma in Italy (Winderman, 2015, p. 48). I traveled to Parma to interview Rizzolatti about this, and after consuming large quantities of incredible cheese and ham, I became fascinated by this story. I also gained several pounds. Researchers on Rizzolatti's team had been conducting experiments on monkeys related to motor neurons, which carry signals from the spinal cord to the muscles to allow for movement. One of Rizzolatti's lab assistants came into the lab one day while eating an ice cream cone. One of the monkeys, who was still wired up to the monitors, craned its head to watch the assistant. On the monitor, the monkey's brain lit up with electrical activity, as if the animal were also eating the ice cream. The primate mimicked the assistant and even moved its arms, mouth, and tongue as though also enjoying the cone.

Rizzolatti's team conducted further research using peanuts and found the same motor neurons fired in the same way whether the monkeys were handling the peanuts or observing others doing so. Subsequent research on humans led to the theory that mirror neurons trigger our brain to simulate the action of those we observe. We can also mimic the emotions we see when expressed by others. We may actually feel the same emotions we witness. This is why people may cry during a sad scene in a movie. I've never done this, don't think for a minute I have.

Neuroscientists like Dr. Rizzolatti believe mirror neurons play an important role in the learning process, which is why storytelling can be powerful. For recruiting, sales, and marketing pros, proper storytelling presents the opportunity to influence a candidate or prospect's mirror neurons to help them emotionally understand and remember the benefits of our offering.

A well-told story activates areas in our brain that allow us to translate the story into our own experiences and concepts. This is called neural coupling. When our brains process facts being told, the Broca and Wernicke areas of our brains are activated, along with our motor, sensory, and frontal cortex.

STORY STRUCTURE

Dr. Paul Zak validated that when we're experiencing a story with a dramatic arc, our brain pumps out two neurochemicals we learned about earlier: oxytocin, the trust hormone that's involved with emotions, love, and bonding, as well as cortisol, the stress hormone that sharpens our powers of concentration. When Zak conducted one experiment, he noted that when participants viewed an emotionally charged father and son story, many of them became more open to charitable donations.

Said Zak, "We discovered that to motivate a desire to help others, a story must first sustain attention—a scarce resource in the brain—by developing tension during the narrative. If the story can create that tension, then it is likely attentive viewers or listeners will come to share the emotions of the characters in it and, after it ends, are likely to continue mimicking the feelings and behaviors of those characters."

Zak also found that effective storytelling structures that better stimulate these neurochemicals include Freytag's Pyramid and the three-act play.

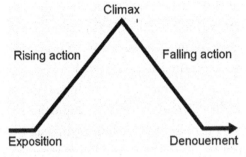

Gustav Freytag was a nineteenth-century German novelist who noticed several common patterns hidden in the plots of well-written stories. He created a diagram depicting a typical structure and used a pyramid to diagram the story plot. Freytag determined that to emotionally engage readers, good stories need to include rising action, a compelling climax, and a satisfying resolution. Gustav's diagram is quite similar to the three-act play made famous by Shakespeare.

3-Act Play Framework

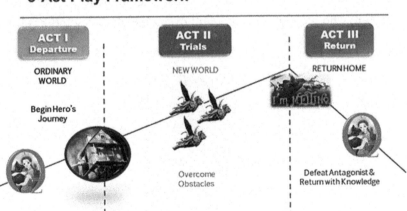

THE HERO'S JOURNEY

In Act I, we need to describe the hero's Ordinary World in colorful (or lack thereof) and visual detail. We should show them as either unhappy or neutral but not yet fulfilling their life's passion and purpose. We then turn up the gas and create a "call to action." This is a situation in which the hero becomes motivated to act. Author Joseph Campbell adapted this ancient format of storytelling, which has underpinned human interaction since the dawn of our species, and delivered it to the world as a monomyth—a pattern that we all recognize and try to emulate in our own life journeys. With the Hero's Journey pattern, one that we've experienced in nearly every book or movie, we start with a hero in a mundane and normal "everyday" life.

Campbell describes the impetus to embark on the Hero's Journey as an act of volition akin to Theseus when he heard about the Minotaur, or Odysseus, who was swept away by a malignant agent, or as a "mere blunder" when our hero stumbles across an event or person that pushes him or her toward the edge. With our prospects, as heroes of their stories, they must mimic Theseus and be willing to undertake an adventure of their own free will. They must be convinced to set aside fear, pride, sloth, repose, and the advice of well-meaning colleagues and risk stepping out of their comfortable worlds. They must learn that a hero is anyone who has survived pain and overcome obstacles and has been transformed by his or her struggles.

The Hero's Journey is also about cause and effect. It's about action and reaction. As noted above, an action, such as a "mere blunder," pushes our hero forward. If there is no action or cause, there is no reaction or effect. Something or someone does or says something that spurs our hero to act. As the story progresses, the hero is constantly reacting to the antagonist, mentor, and/or situations they face in order to complete their journey. This creates a vital ying-yang effect to propel the story forward.

ACT I

In Act I of the three-act play, we begin by immersing our audience into the Ordinary World as described in the Hero's Journey format. Great writers understand that it's critical within the first few pages of a book to grab the reader's attention and connect with them emotionally. The operative word here is "emotionally." In this act, we need to primarily appeal to the emotional part of our brain. Says leading neuroscientist Dr. Garcia-Fresco, "Emotions are stored in your memory centers together with the events that triggered those emotions. The more emotional events we experience in life, the more memories we form. Subconsciously our decisions are influenced by stored events and the emotions they elicit. Our brains love patterns. If we have a memory of an event that triggered a happy response, whenever we encounter a similar event, our brain will subconsciously guide us to make a decision so that it can enjoy that happy feeling again."

Triggering emotional responses and grabbing immediate attention requires knowing how to open and close scenes. I was fortunate to receive some excellent training on this from a true master. Joan Johnston is the *New York Times* bestselling author of over forty novels, including the *Bitter Creek* and *Hawk's Way* series, with over ten million copies in print. She taught me eight ways to keep readers turning pages by using proven techniques to start and end scenes and chapters. Let's learn what these are, and later on we'll see how we can use them for almost anything we write or present, including emails, messages, phone scripts, white papers, success stories, blogs, solution briefs, and even PowerPoint presentations. We'll also explore how they can be very effective when opening and closing sales or recruiting conversations.

The eight techniques are:

1. Asking a question for which the audience wants an answer
2. Creating a crisis, threat, or unsolvable problem
3. Anticipating a confrontation or clash, verbal or physical, between characters
4. Riveting or compelling action that causes unusual behavior
5. Anticipating what will happen when someone learns a secret
6. Setting a contest, competition, or bargain to be met
7. Forecasting a disaster that can only be avoided by some action
8. Setting a deadline for a decision or action, such as an ultimatum

Writers refer to these tactics as "hooks" and know they are vital in gaining reader attention within the first few seconds. If we don't do this well, attention and eyes will wander and readers will put down a book. In sales, recruiting, and marketing scenarios, prospects or candidates will start texting or fidgeting or delete a document, and we'll lose them…and the opportunity. Once hooked, we can pull our audience into Act I and captivate them with our titillating story.

There are three phases in the Hero's Journey, which coincide with the three-act play: departure, struggle, and return. When the protagonist or hero walks onto the stage in the Act I departure phase, top storytellers use several techniques to create a "sympathetic character." If we don't care about our hero, we won't care whether they succeed or fail. Top writers often use an associative technique to do this.

James Rollins is the #1 *New York Times* bestselling novelist of the *Sigma* series and numerous other thrillers. He and I frequently team up to teach audiences the science and structure of storytelling. He often fashions characters with two or three of the following seven qualities to create sympathetic protagonists:

- Top of their game—"black belt" in their craft
- Funny, humorous, entertaining
- Kind, caring, treats others well
- Shows kindness to pets, kids, or the elderly
- Has endured undeserved misfortune
- Others like them or show them love
- They have physical, mental, or educational handicaps

It's best not to use *all* of these for a single character, lest we create coffee with too much sugar. In the book *The Wonderful Wizard of Oz* by L. Frank Baum, during Act I, Dorothy shows kindness to elderly relatives and her dog, and others show love toward her. This is enough for us to care about her and to want to defend her when the flying monkeys start attacking.

Also in Act I, Baum does a masterful job of painting a vivid picture of Dorothy's Ordinary World, describing it in the same fashion he does for any other character on the stage:

> *When Dorothy stood in the doorway and looked around, she could see nothing but the great gray prairie on every side. Not a tree nor a house broke the broad sweep of flat country that reached to the edge of the sky in all directions. The sun had baked the plowed land into a gray mass, with little cracks running through it. Even the grass was not green, for the sun had burned the tops of the long blades until they were the same gray color to be seen everywhere. Once the house had been painted, but the sun blistered the paint and the rains washed it away, and now the house was as dull and gray as everything else.*

We see and *feel* the gray and dusty landscape and *feel* as Dorothy does, unfulfilled but not yet willing to leave her comfort zone. Dorothy was obviously not happy in her gray world, but she was also reluctant to leave because, after all, it was her home. In truth, it was not the dull house or gray land that Dorothy dreaded; it was the perception of the Ordinary World she had created between her own two ears. In truth, she was unhappy with herself but reluctant to leave.

In Act I, Baum also reveals Dorothy's initial wants and desires. This is called the MacGuffin, which is the object of her quest. The MacGuffin is a fictional object invented by Alfred Hitchcock. It's the "thing" that all the primary characters in a story are trying to obtain or keep, such as the ring in *The Lord of the Rings*. They all see it as the means to their end. If they can get the MacGuffin, it will bring them closer to their true desires. If Rocky can win the big fight, he can have the life he's always wanted. If Luke can destroy the Death Star, he can help save the universe, and so on.

While showing us Dorothy's desires, Baum also ensures that every scene in the book includes conflict. This is essential to any great story and requires antagonists. There should be a singular opposing bad dude, or dudette, but there should also be several baddie minions. In Baum's book, Dorothy's initial conflict is internal. She is battling her boredom in her gray world. Baum injects more conflict when the tornado picks up Dorothy's house and frightens her and Toto. Then he escalates the conflicts and the tension.

Our hero is also flawed in some way. They have faults, issues, bad habits, failures, insecurities, or in Dorothy's case, a lack of vision. She does not see or appreciate what she already has. She must face obstacles, tests, trials, and failures through her Act II journey before she can recognize and overcome these shortcomings. However, she can't begin this journey until thrust into Act II.

As noted earlier, Act I should be about 25 percent of our story.

CONCLUSIONS

- Stories make us cry and increase our retention by 1400 percent, which is a lot.
- Most stories have three acts—the beginning, middle, and end—and they make us cry.
- Dorothy was bored in Kansas, which is typical for most people who live in Kansas (just kidding).

CHAPTER 9

FLYING MONKEYS

*"Don't worry about the world coming to an end
today. It is already tomorrow in Australia."*
—Charles M. Schulz

ACT II

The hero usually refuses the call to depart from their Ordinary World in Act I, before they step into the new world in Act II. It's natural for them to be reluctant, to question whether a new path is right, or to wonder if they should take any risks at all. If their pain or desire is not high enough yet to overcome trepidation or to motivate them to do something to attain the outcome they want, they will take no action. However, if their desire *is* high enough, they can be persuaded to muster the courage to step outside comfort zones and depart on their journey. Cause and effect now comes into play, wherein our hero reacts to situations, such as being whisked away to the land of Oz. Or…the prompting and actions delivered by the antagonist or mentor, such as the Wizard of Oz sending Dorothy and her friends on a quest.

If you're wondering how this relates to a selling or recruiting situation, imagine your prospect or candidate in their Ordinary World, reluctant to step out of their comfort zone and try something new.

The conflict and the stakes are smaller in Act I but still present. With Dorothy, they are mostly internal as she is unfulfilled in her Ordinary World. Tension and stakes ramp with the tornado and the death of the Wicked Witch of the East as we cross into Act II. While the Munchkins are thrilled, Dorothy is wrought with conflict, as shown when she cried, "Oh, dear! Oh, dear!" and clasped her hands together.

Dorothy did not choose to have her house and dog tossed over the rainbow and land in Oz…on top of a bad witch. Given a choice, she likely would have turned down the offer. Most often, a mentor encourages the hero to move beyond their comfort zone and begin an adventure or quest. The hero will not, *cannot* do this until they meet and trust their mentor, either in the latter part of Act I or early part of Act II. In the Act II struggle portion of the Hero's Journey, our hero must be challenged. Doing this requires speaking to the instinctual brain in the right way.

As we learned previously, the emotional and instinctual parts of our brain are visual, sensual, and tactile. Great writers, like Baum, deftly engage all our senses when they craft scenes. Baum wrote *The Wonderful Wizard of Oz* in 1900, long before neuroscience came to light. Still, like Aristotle, he knew the value of touching all our senses. Sight, sound, smell, taste, and feel. As noted earlier, scientists now understand why the word "rose" taps the part of our brain that reminds us of how this flower smells. When Dorothy lands in Oz, Baum describes her new world in vivid detail.

> *There were lovely patches of greensward all about, with stately trees bearing rich and luscious fruits. Banks of gorgeous flowers were on every hand, and birds with rare and brilliant plumage sang and fluttered in the trees and bushes. A little way off was a small brook, rushing and sparkling along between green banks, and murmuring in a voice very grateful to a little girl who had lived so long on the dry, gray prairies.*

Baum also triggers another key human sense to keep his readers on the edge of their seats: curiosity. While not often referred to as one of our "senses," it is definitely an innate human trait. Scientists now understand the reason we're so curious is because our brain rewards us for this behavior. Researchers discovered that the brain's reward chemical, dopamine, is intricately linked to our brain's curiosity state. We feel good when our curiosity leads to learning and knowing. If our curiosity is high enough, we're *driven* to know. Keep this fact in your back pocket, as light bulbs will be ignited on this topic in later chapters. Curious yet?

Baum intrigues us by doling out tidbits of information that make us curious about Oz and its inhabitants. He does this by having Dorothy ask questions, and by having the Good Witch of the North provide only partial answers. When one of the Munchkins calls Dorothy a sorceress, she wonders (asks):

> *What could the little woman possibly mean by calling her a sorceress, and saying she had killed the Wicked Witch of the East?*

Dorothy then asks the Good Witch questions about Oz and this mysterious wizard. The witch leaves her, and us, curious by offering just enough information to whet our appetite. For example, she tells Dorothy that the silver shoes (ruby in the movie) worn by the dried-up Wicked Witch of the East are now hers. She picks them up, shakes off the dirt, and hands them to Dorothy. Then one of the Munchkins peaks our curiosity even further:

> *"The Witch of the East was proud of those silver shoes,"*
> *said one of the Munchkins, "and there is some charm con-*
> *nected with them; but what it is we never knew."*

The Good Witch delivers a few more morsels to keep us interested and then points Dorothy toward the Emerald City. Still early in Act II, Dorothy, like most heroes, refuses the call to embark on her quest. She asks how she might find her way back home and is told by the Good Witch that no one knows, so she must remain in Oz.

> *Dorothy began to sob at this, for she felt lonely among all*
> *these strange people.*

Left with no choice, she finds the courage to follow the yellow brick road to the Emerald City to find the Wizard. Along the way, she meets our tin guy, timid lion, and not so smart scarecrow. They find the Wizard, of course, who becomes their mentor and sends them on a quest to retrieve the Wicked Witch's broom. In exchange, he'll grant their wishes. The broom, at first, becomes the MacGuffin, but we later discover it's actually the silver (ruby) slippers. The Witch wants them, making Dorothy curious as to why.

By now, you're probably wondering what any of this has to do with recruiting, selling, business, or marketing. The answer is, *everything*. In the next chapter, all the pieces will come together and we'll see why our prospect or candidate is Dorothy and we are the Wizard. For now, it's important to gain a foundational understanding of story structure and techniques before we can properly employ them, so let's journey onward.

In Act II, James Rollins tells us we must do the following to raise tension and stakes.

- Torture the hero and their co-protagonists
- Create nearly insurmountable roadblocks

- Escalate tension by making the challenges harder
- Have the hero and antagonist exchange winning and losing
- Show how the hero cares about someone, then place that person in danger

Diana Gabaldon is a master at all the above. I believe she ran a torture chamber in an earlier life. Her *Outlander* books—now a television series—have been read by millions. In nearly every scene, she tortures her characters beyond belief. How anyone can endure what they go through is mind boggling, and because she ensures readers care about and are invested in her protagonists, we frantically turn pages. This plot device is critical to storytelling, and separates great writers from mediocre ones. It's the difference between a *New York Times* bestselling novel and one sold only to relatives. It's also the difference between successful recruiting, sales, and marketing pros and ones who never get promoted.

Achieving this difference requires guts. We writers become attached to our characters. We conceived them, brought them to life, and journeyed with them through hell. It's not easy to make them suffer. Doing so takes courage, but if we handle them with kid gloves, they will never be tested, never grow up, and never fulfill their Hero's Journey. It's a lot like the relationship we parents with have with our children. If we're "helicopter parents" and always shield our kids from the perils of life, they'll remain dependent upon us and unable to tackle life's struggles on their own. On the other hand, what parent isn't anguished when their kid starts crying?

Again, you may be wondering how this relates to business. Also again, all will soon be revealed, but here's a hint: *The Challenger Sale.* The authors of this book, while perhaps misclassifying types of salespersons, were correct in noting that those who challenge customer beliefs are more successful. If your customer is the hero, how hard is it to torture them by challenging their beliefs?

As James Rollins points out, Act II of our story should have a ying-yang back-and-forth flow. Visualize the diagonal tension line running from one edge of the paper, upward to the beginning of Act III. Along this line, imagine another zigzag line frequently going above and below. This is your tension line. Now imagine a great sports event, such as a football game. In all stories, your hero and antagonist should be equally matched, with the antagonist having a slight edge. In our football game, our visiting team is an underdog and in the first quarter of the game, the better opponent scores a touchdown and our team only scores a field goal. The score is seven to three. Through the next two quarters, the game goes back and forth. We cheer when our team pulls ahead and bite our lips when they fall behind, but this back-and-forth tension makes for a thrilling ride. Finally, in the fourth quarter, we're down by six points and time is running out. Will our team score a touchdown and win? Our hearts pound and our palms sweat as we stand and cheer for a miracle. Now that's a story!

We were tortured, along with our team, for almost three hours during this game, but we loved every minute of it. Perhaps we're all sick puppies, but that's how we're wired. We love underdogs, we love to see our heroes challenged and come out ahead, and we love great stories.

Maintaining tension requires understanding the difference between surprise and suspense. James Rollins describes surprise as two people sitting at a table in a café when a bomb goes off nearby. We're surprised or shocked. Suspense is when someone places the bomb under the table. We know it's there, but the two characters in this scene do not. They're talking casually while we're biting our nails. Will they leave before the bomb goes off?

Most often the hero must face the villain, the more powerful antagonist, on her turf. This raises the stakes. Our team does not get to play at home. They must win the big game on the road at the opponent's stadium. The bad guy must always have the advantage. How often have we seen the hero get hurt right before the final fight, game, or contest? They were already an underdog, and became even more so right before the climax.

Dorothy and her companions must face the Wicked Witch in the castle. To obtain the broom, which they perceive as the MacGuffin, they must sneak in and take it. As a child, every time I watched the movie,

I shivered with fright. Already knowing the outcome did not lessen my trepidation. I still felt like the frightened lion tiptoeing into the Witch's castle. The sound of those guards chanting with a deep baritone still makes me cower to this day.

Surprise is also a necessary element in Act II. Right before the climax, after the halfway point in Act II, we should deliver an unexpected "surprise" plot twist. Just when readers believe they have the story figured out, great writers surprise them with a direction shift. In *The Wonderful Wizard of Oz*, the Wicked Witch of the West discovers that the silver (ruby) slippers cannot be removed from Dorothy's feet without her permission. The only way the Witch can get them is to end Dorothy's life. Obviously, we're *surprised* and terrified by this plot twist.

In this climactic scene, when the sands in the hourglass are about to run out, we feel as Dorothy does: like failures. We faced our ultimate test and did not pass. The evil Witch won. To make this moment even more stressful, experienced writers use another familiar trick: they take even more time away from the hero. When our protagonist is trying to defuse the nuclear bomb and the digital timer shows less than five minutes, they clip the wrong wire and the timer jumps ahead to only one minute. Our hearts beat even faster as the timer speeds toward the last second. Finally, our hero clips the correct wire and saves the day.

Again, you might be wondering how this or anything else in this chapter pertains to business situations. Recall the initial story in this book, where Linda informed John that, due to unforeseen circumstances, he had even less time than previously thought before disaster struck. John's heart beat faster, and he was even more motivated to take immediate action.

While in the castle, with the sand in the hourglass running thin, Dorothy digs deep into her soul and finds the courage she had all along. Angered, she throws water on the Witch, who melts into a puddle of ooze. All that's left is the broom.

Dorothy grabs the broom—her *perceived* MacGuffin—and steps into Act III.

Act II should be about 50 percent of our story and usually ends with the climax. Some writers place the climax at the beginning of Act III, which can also work if done correctly.

CONCLUSIONS

- To tell a good story, you must torture people.
- When someone tries to secretly blow you up, it's called suspense.
- Everyone wants the MacGuffin, which can sometimes look like a broom.

ACT III

All great stories have a theme. It's the overall message the author wants to deliver to the reader. In the Act III return phase of the journey, our hero returns to their Ordinary World with the "magic elixir." It's most often the wisdom or knowledge gained by the hero. They have completed their character's arc. If we look back, we can recall the hero's flaws in Act I. We can now see they have overcome these by facing their Act II trials and tests. They are now ready to share the wisdom they have gained with others in their Ordinary World. Dorothy discovers that she had the ability to return home anytime she wanted. The question asked by a Munchkin in Act II about the East Witch's silver (ruby) slippers—the one that piqued our curiosity—is finally answered. We now know why the Wicked Witch of the West wanted those slippers. They're magical. They, and the not the broom, were the true MacGuffin. Dorothy only needed to click her heels together and wish for home.

Back in Kansas, Dorothy has newfound wisdom. She acknowledges her flaws, her lack of vision and inability to appreciate what she already had, and imparts the story's theme in a single sentence: "There's no place like home."

James Rollins advises us to have a logical ending. We're all familiar with Act III in a Sherlock Holmes story. Our hero logically brings all the fuzzy facts together in the end. The seemingly unconnected puzzle pieces fall into place as he skillfully forms a picture of the killer and his motives. We're educated and entertained by the "ah ha" moment and smile while turning the final page.

Act III, obviously, should be about 25 percent of our story and leave us satisfied.

Now that we're masterful storytellers, let's learn how to use our skills to win customer or candidate hearts and minds in the Ordinary World of business.

CONCLUSIONS

- There's no place like home, which happens to be in a Kansas "theme" park.
- The ending to any story should be logical, as if told by a guy with pointed ears.
- The puzzle pieces should fit together nicely, not like a three-year-old did it.

CHAPTER 10
FROG ACTS

"I used to sell furniture for a living.
The trouble was, it was my own."
—Les Dawson

A s promised, in the next few chapters, many of your curiosity questions will now be answered. We'll learn how to apply our newfound storytelling superpowers in recruiting, sales, marketing, and business scenarios. To simplify our visualizations, we'll use a diagram, an acronym, a success story, and a PowerPoint presentation as examples. For the latter, I'll show you how to convey almost *any* concept by using only *four images* and *twelve bullet points*. Gone are the days of fifty-slide presentations with 50,000 bullets. Beyond presentations and success stories, proper storytelling techniques can also be applied within web pages, white papers, blogs, customer conversations, or whatever.

While most readers may prefer in-depth storytelling knowledge and details, others may desire more simplicity. For example, a sales engineer named Adam, at a client technology firm, needed to create a training course for the sales team. Adam had constructed the typical "speeds and feeds" presentation with dozens of tech terms, data, numbers, facts, percentages, and concepts. His intentions were good, but his approach would have caused serious eye rolling from the sales team. In a Zoom call, to simplify his task, I asked Adam to use a sheet of paper turned sideways in landscape view. Then, I had him draw three lines to create four equal segments. These represented the four story segments, which we now know are labeled Act I, Act IIa, Act IIb, and Act III. Again, as Act II is about 50 percent of our story, we divided this into two segments representing 25 percent each.

Starting from the left, I asked Adam to write one of these words in each segment: Focus, Risks, Obstacles, and Gains, with Focus in Act I, Risks in Act IIa, and so on. This spells FROG and represents the actions and prompting of the mentor. As we are the mentor in our prospect's story, FROG helps us remember what we should *do* to create "cause and effect." Also starting from left to right, I asked Adam to write these words in each segment: Adequate, Concerned, Tense, and Satisfied. This spells the acronym ACTS, which represents how our prospect should *respond* to our prompting. Before moving on, take a few minutes to say FROG ACTS at least a dozen times so it becomes so memorable it endlessly plays in your head like Disney's *It's a Small World After All*.

FROG ACTS Messaging Framework

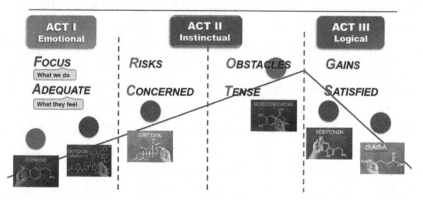

I asked Adam to imagine an IT director named John. In Act I, we need to *focus* on his *adequate* situation. We need to prompt our hero to help us understand how he feels. John spent years learning and understanding dozens of technologies and solutions. He spent long months studying to get a half-dozen technical certifications. He applied all this knowledge to his situation, and for the moment, he feels fine. He knows his firm can always do better, but he doesn't believe he has any current problems that require immediate action. His situation is adequate.

In Act IIa, I instructed Adam that we need to ask more questions and impart *risk* information so John the prospect begins to feel *concerned*. Our prompting should help John open his eyes to the truth and prompt him to take action. Either his firm has been attacked by hackers or we educate him about an unknown and urgent threat—perhaps a new ransomware strain. John then realizes that his situation is no longer adequate. He raises an eyebrow, leans forward, and listens.

In Act IIb, we help John understand the *obstacles* he must overcome to avoid the negative impact of inaction or wrong action. John should feel *tense* as we tell him a story about another customer who ignored the warnings and suffered severe consequences. Naturally, John does not want this to happen to his firm. He squirms in his seat. We illustrate a "what if" scenario designed to overcome or avoid the obstacle, and John is hopeful that this might offer a way to vanquish his foes. Our prompting helps nudge John forward into the next act.

In Act III, we can impart the *gains* of taking action to make the right decision to use our solutions to defeat the antagonist. John should feel *satisfied* with this decision. However, he can't complete his Hero's Journey until he brings home the magic elixir. He must deliver his newfound knowledge to others in his Ordinary World. Why is this important? Studies show that in a complex sale, most of the "selling" occurs *after* salespersons exit the room. The best sales and marketing pros know they must create evangelists who will sell on their behalf. John may have a dozen individuals at his firm who must also be sold, and it's virtually impossible for any vendor to meet with or influence all of them. For recruiters, "others" might be the candidate's spouse, a colleague, or close friend. They too need to be sold on John's potential career change.

Recall the television show *Home Improvement* with Tim Allen, where Mr. Wilson, from across the fence, imparted knowledge to Tim to help him with family problems. Tim never got it right. He always distorted the facts when telling his wife or others what he'd learned. We want to avoid this, of course, which requires imparting information to John that he can remember and repeat. In the opening story in this book, Linda did this by giving John a document she called an ARC—a cheat sheet John could use to "sell" other decision-makers at his firm on the value propositions provided by Linda's solutions. We'll review this in more depth later on, but for now, let's recall what we've learned.

What my colleague Adam discovered is that for any presentation, written document, or sales scenario, we label our four story segments with Focus and Adequate, Risks and Concerned, Obstacles and Tense, and Gains and Satisfied (FROG ACTS). We can then create scripts and content appropriate for each section. In Act I, we should ask questions and offer information relevant to a prospect's Ordinary World situation. We should not yet explore problems or issues until Act IIa. There, we can ask more questions to understand the prospect's perceived concerns. We need to impart a risk story that illustrates similar issues faced by a customer and how they ignored the warnings, which led to consequences.

This transitions us into Act IIb, where we explore the impact of inaction or wrong action. What obstacles were faced by the customer in the story we told, and what might it cost our prospect if they make no decision or a bad decision? Our prospect should feel tense. This sets up Act III, where we use "what if" scenarios to outline the gains delivered by our solutions. "What if we could avoid these consequences with…" Our prospect should feel satisfied as we bring our story to a close by offering three logical choices: no action, wrong action, optimal action. We now use facts, figures, and return on investment (ROI) data to validate why no action and wrong action are too costly. We use similar data to show why optimal action—our solution—is the best choice.

Telling a proper story can be that simple, but if you want to master this art, please stop texting and keep reading. As you may have already surmised, the acronym FROG is a double entendre. It helps remind us to avoid focusing on analytical data that appeals only to the logical brain, and also to heed Aristotle's advice to speak to all three areas, most importantly the instinctual brain. As we recall, this brain is often referred to as the reptilian brain, and while frogs are amphibians, they *look* a bit like reptiles. Again, ACTS focuses on how our prospects *feel*, FROG represents what we as business professionals should *do* in each story segment to create cause and effect. In Act I, we should focus on the prospect's Ordinary World and seek to understand their situation. In Act IIa, we need to uncover and reveal problems and concerns that pose risks. In Act IIb, we must discuss the impact these may have on the prospect and the obstacles they must overcome to avoid serious consequences. In Act III, we can offer gains for making the right decision.

In summary, simply remember how a FROG ACTS by visualizing croaking, leaping, and eating flies. In our case, after the prospect croaks, we can help them leap out of their Ordinary World, complete their journey, and finally return home to enjoy a satisfied life while eating flies and sitting on a lily pad.

BUILDING TRUST

We know that two of our initial goals when presenting a story are to position ourselves as mentors and our candidates, prospects, or customers as heroes. We also know that most often, a mentor encourages the hero to move beyond their comfort zone and begin an adventure or quest. In the Act I concerned and focus segment, salespersons, marketers, recruiters, and leaders assume the role of the mentor. Our task is to help our hero (prospect) gain the courage to step into the Act IIa concerned risks segment. They will not, *cannot* do this until they trust us. To trust us, they must first like us. Millions of years of biology have wired the human brain to discern either friend or foe. Once we are perceived as a friend, we can build trust. Once we've built trust, we can help our hero follow us through the Act IIa concerned risks and Act IIb tense obstacles segments and eventually into the Act III satisfied gains segment.

Let's examine how we can create cause and effect in each act to build trust and propel the Hero's Journey forward…

ACT I: ADEQUATE FOCUS

Whenever I tell a story to persuade a customer to take action, my goal in Act I is to primarily use Aristotle's Ethos techniques to persuade someone's emotional brain. Dopamine, of course, is a type of neurotransmitter that helps trigger happy, emotional responses. Our bodies naturally produce this in our nervous systems and use it to send messages between our nerve cells. That's why some neuroscientists call it a chemical messenger. Dopamine plays an important role in why and how we feel pleasure and helps us focus, engage, and maintain interest.

In Act I, we begin by understanding our Hero's Ordinary World as described in the Hero's Journey format. As we now know, great writers understand it's critical within the first few pages of a book to grab the reader's attention and connect with them emotionally. We need to tug on heartstrings and create "sympathetic characters."

In *The Challenger Sale*, the initial step is called the warmer. I guess the authors didn't spend much time on creating cool terms. The Sandler submarine compartments start with bonding and rapport. SPIN Selling calls the first step the opening, and so on. Virtually all frameworks open the door in similar fashion. They suggest asking for the PO right away. Okay seriously, and in contrast to the age-old ABC approach that advises us to Always Be Closing, every top sales and marketing pro knows we first need to establish a relationship. Even strong-willed Challenger types must begin this way if they want to get past first base. Let's examine our top three trust builders:

- Create a sympathetic Hero prospect
- Tell a sympathetic hero story
- Become a sympathetic mentor

Strong and "in control" Challenger types might wrinkle their nose at the word "sympathetic." Sure sounds a lot like that "loser" Relationship Builder guy. Perhaps, but again, even *The Challenger Sale* recommends being nice during the warmer phase. Let's review again the seven techniques used by James Rollins to create sympathetic characters:

- Top of their game—black belt in their craft
- Funny, humorous, entertaining
- Kind, caring, treats others well
- Shows kindness to pets, kids, or the elderly
- Has endured undeserved misfortune
- Others like them or show them love
- They have physical, mental, or educational handicaps

When engaging with customers, we can use a few of these techniques to increase dopamine and ensure prospects like us...

- Ask a prospect to talk about themselves and their "black belt" ability and create a sympathetic hero prospect by showing them we understand they are the protagonist of *their* story.

- Tell a sympathetic hero "success" story and help our prospect see us as kind mentors by showing how we helped other protagonists kill an evil witch.
- Become an entertaining and wise mentor "great Oz" to ensure our prospect likes and trusts us enough to grant us more than a minute.

Our emotional brain is more visual, so we need to refrain from using lots of copy, facts, figures, and graphs. Says Dr. Garcia-Fresco, "We are very visual creatures. We process visual inputs much faster than anything else, hence a visual image can elicit a quicker decision. You can use storytelling to paint a picture of a present memory in their minds, which will most likely trigger the resurgence of a similar memory they had or even create a new pleasant one."

Here's an example of how we might open a conversation to accomplish our Act I goals and create a sympathetic hero:

We start with the usual introductions: "Hi, I'm Linda and you're John."

We now deliver a brief statement of why we're here and the goal of the meeting, followed immediately with a question to get John talking about himself. We might say, "I'm here today to learn more about your situation and discuss how we can help you solve issues related to your cybersecurity posture, but first, I'd like to learn more about you and your background. How did you become the director of IT here, and what does your current role entail?"

Everyone loves to talk about themselves, and when we allow them to do so while showing genuine interest, we accomplish three important things:

- We learn more about who they are and how to communicate with them.
- We position them as the hero of their story.
- We help them *like* us, and therefore *trust* us as a mentor.

Once John has spent a few hours bragging about himself, we can ask more situational questions, such as why he likes the Raiders and not the 49ers. Okay, maybe not *that* question, but you get the idea. Again, in Act I, we should not ask about problems or discuss implications. Our questions should remain neutral and seek to understand more about John's Ordinary World. Imagine you're having a conversation with a friend you haven't seen in a while. You would not ask them why their daughter married an unemployed moron that rides a motorcycle without a helmet and has a hundred tattoos. Nope, you'd first ask how things are going, did they remodel their kitchen, get a new hairstylist, etc. What's going on in your obviously boring life, Mary?

As we recall, Baum does not yet challenge Dorothy until later in Act I, when she is tossed by a tornado into Act II. Likewise, and unlike actions prescribed by Nancy Duarte in her VisualStories workshops, we should not discuss problems in Act I. In Neil Rackham's SPIN Selling, the "S" stands for "situation." This is Act I. We are focused on the prospect's situation in their Ordinary World. We are therefore more focused on emotions and feelings. How does our hero *feel* about Kansas? How does his business operate? What solutions is he using? We are asking him questions to better understand his needs and wants and to set up problems and implications (the P and I in SPIN) later in Act II.

Marketers can also get prospects to "talk about themselves" and reveal information about their Ordinary World by having them self-select and answer a few questions. Using the power of three, we might have a website with three questions, such as Novice? Intermediate? Experienced? Each selection takes visitors to a landing page with information pertinent to the prospect's persona and experience level. There, we can ask more qualifying questions to funnel them to the right solutions and presentations.

Now let's sprinkle in some sympathetic character techniques. With our example, Linda might say, "John, your background is quite extensive and I'm impressed by how quickly you became the director of IT here. You're obviously adept at making smart decisions."

By complimenting John on being at the top of his game, Linda has positioned him as the sympathetic hero in his story. Note how she also mentioned that he makes smart decisions. This is an example of a "setup statement" she can use later in Act II. Here's a sneak peek: "John, your background validates that you're obviously adept at making smart decisions, so don't be an idiot and make a bad choice that will cause your firm to go bankrupt and put you in a breadline."

Obviously, I'm going a bit over the top here, but recall how Socrates used deductive reasoning. He asked a series of no-brainer "yes" questions followed by a closing question that had to be answered with a yes. We can also do this with "yes" statements, such as the one Linda just used. "You're obviously adept at making smart decisions, *right*?" If John says, "Nope, I always make really bad decisions," then he's probably not your best prospect.

Now that we've stimulated dopamine and positioned our prospect as a sympathetic character and us as a sympathetic and likable mentor, we can start building trust. As we learned earlier, this requires increasing brain oxytocin. Dr. Garcia-Fresco has written about building trust in numerous articles and books. In an interview, he says, "Every top sales and marketing professional knows that 90 percent of customers buy on trust, but what they may not know is that oxytocin is the key. This brain chemical helps us trust. If it's low, we will be skeptical and untrusting. If high, we will like or love someone, and therefore be more inclined to trust them."

This is also important to know for business leaders. Dr. Paul Zak spent years validating that high-trust organizations with trusted and trusting employees drive far higher energy, productivity, and profits. Recruiters should seek to employ people who exhibit high trust capabilities. More on this later.

We trust our friends, and at first may mistrust strangers. Some people trust everyone, even if they're wearing a plastic mask and holding a chain saw, but since they usually don't live long, these genes are rarely passed on. All kidding aside, as noted by Dr. Zak, there are dozens of ways to increase oxytocin. To ensure simplicity, as related to business situations, let's narrow these down to three primary trust builders.

By asking John a few—and I do mean a *few*—situational questions in a friendly way, we can lay the foundation for trust by telling him a sympathetic hero story. For example, Linda might say, "John, your situation sounds similar to Bob Jones, a CIO at XYZ Company. They also had…" Linda then tells a story that offers an illustration of John's situation. This lets John know that Linda was listening and shows him that she and her firm understand his situation. Linda can be trusted, as she and her company have helped someone else with a similar scenario. Again, Linda is not yet discussing problems, only situations.

Linda can further position herself as a trusted advisor by framing her questions with brief—*very brief*—thought-leadership "reframe" information. While being careful to maintain humility, Linda can show John how she is at the top of *her* game. This does not mean she should impart a list of company accolades, such as all the awards her firm has won. Her company is not the hero of John's story. Without dumbing down questions so far as to appear manipulative, Linda can ask a few "yes" questions here to move John out of his comfort zone. For example, she might say, "John, you mentioned having a security product, but you have not yet installed a more advanced solution. You also mentioned having security policies that leverage the latest cybersecurity frameworks. I'm sure you know that the best frameworks recommend a more advanced solution to prevent attacks, right?

While some jerks will mess with Linda and say "No!" nearly all will say yes, lest they appear to be stupid. If John is aware of the latest information, he will be more trusting of Linda, as she appears knowledgeable. If he's not, Linda has just "taught" him something valuable and positioned herself as a wise and trustable Oz. This is a more effective way to "reframe" by imparting a credible fact and then encouraging the prospect to agree by saying yes. Now Linda will have one "yes" in her pocket and can seek to gain at least two more because our brains think in threes, right?

I'll bet you just said yes.

With practice, so we don't sound like a braggart, we can learn how to be a wise mentor that guides our prospect away from his adequate situation in Act I and nudges him toward concerned in Act II. Again, this is the best way to "reframe," as *The Challenger Sale* suggests. Rather than force prospects to see things our way, we should gently open their eyes by using the Socrates "yes" approach. We should also sprinkle in some humor and always treat our prospect with kindness. Contrary to prevailing thought, our aim is to build a friendly (dopamine) and trusting (oxytocin) relationship with our prospect or audience.

In review, we have three goals in Act I:

- Create a sympathetic prospect hero
  By asking them to talk about themselves

- Describe a sympathetic example hero
  By delivering a success story similar to our hero's situation

- Become a sympathetic and trusted mentor
  By asking questions, imparting information, and using the Socrates approach to gain 3+ yeses

The final point above, as noted earlier, is contrary to popular belief that we should only ask open-ended questions. We will ask more of these in Act II, but in Act I, we need to also use deductive reasoning to gain several "yes" closed-ended responses to set up more open-ended questions we will ask later.

I recommend against using a slide presentation in your first prospect meeting but instead only have a conversation similar to the one just described. However, some companies insist on death by PowerPoint. If so, it's best to at least wait until later in Act I, on the cusp of Act II, before whipping open your PC or iPad. Once we've completed our "warmer" intro and have started to "reframe" our prospect's thinking, we can decide if a presentation is warranted. If one is needed, we should keep it short and sweet and use it to prompt more interaction rather than as a way to do all the talking.

On slide 1, many experts insist on having an agenda. I recommend against this. When we pick up a nonfiction book, how many of us spend time studying the contents section? We want to jump right into the text and be captivated. No, you don't need to tell your prospect what your "goal" might be. They already know your goal is to convince them to take action. By starting with bullet point "facts" about what we're going to discuss, we engage their logical brain. Instead, we need to stimulate their emotional brain by immediately pulling them into our story.

Again, we are not the hero of their story, so in the same way we refrained from bragging about ourselves earlier in Act I, let's also not use company accolade slides in the beginning of our presentation. Far too many presentations start with an awards slide with company facts and figures, customer logos, industry accolades, ad nauseam. Please don't do this—you'll embarrass yourself in public.

For your PowerPoint, or whatever presentation program you're using, you may be cordially compelled by your employer to use a standard and boring corporate cover page. Perhaps it's dark blue with swirls and a long cerebral title. If you're allowed to, it's best to use an intriguing picture that not only summarizes what your prospect will learn but raises their curiosity. If not allowed to do this by the stodgy powers that be, hopefully you can at least create a short eyebrow-raising curiosity title such as:

Ransomware Revelations

Why we're losing the war against cybercrime

This is similar to titles often used for nonfiction books. The main title is short and catchy, similar to a subject line in an email. The subtitle is also short but more explanatory, such as the subhead in an email.

The second slide should have a picture of "John," our hero in the story we're unfolding. John can be a fictional character, or someone real if we have permission to use an actual success story. If at all possible, our story should be based on a true story. John or Joan, as the hero, should be on the left side of the first slide. We're visual and we read from left to right (unless you're in China). You want your audience to *first* see a picture of the hero (going from left to right) and not black-and-white copy. You can sashay this back and forth on subsequent slides, but it's best to start with a hero image on the left. John or Joan should be smiling, but only partially. He or she should not be wearing a suit but instead be smartly dressed in business casual light blue, yellow, or green clothing. He has his arms crossed and appears skeptical. Behind him, the Ordinary World should not be colorful. Instead, it should be as gray and dull as Dorothy's Kansas.

On the right side, use only three short bullet points. For example:

John is an IT Director.

He installed endpoint security.

He thought he was protected from ransomware...

While still in Act I, what part of the brain are we primarily addressing? Now that we're trained neuroscientists, this answer should be academic, Watson. If you answered logical neocortex, you are incorrect and have failed this course. Please put down your pencil and exit the classroom. You will later be humiliated on Facebook.

As I'm sure you answered limbic system, or emotional brain, you are correct. What primary neurotransmitter and brain chemical are we therefore stimulating? Dopamine and oxytocin, of course. What colors should we use? Light blues, greens, yellows, and pastels. Our visuals should be bright, friendly, and inviting. As noted, pictures should show someone with a slight but not yet beaming smile. We want a sympathetic character, not yet a fulfilled and thrilled customer or candidate. For salespersons or recruiters, vocal timbre can make or break you. The same is true for written words. What should your tone (for voice and copy) be in Act I? Also bright, friendly, and inviting. In addition, knowledgeable without sounding snooty.

Pacing can be vital to storytelling, so what should it be in Act I? *Moderate.* Not too fast and not too slow. We don't want to bore our audience, but we're not yet ready to move at breakneck speed. Stay in the middle. Always use active verbs, but after asking questions, take the time to listen, nod, and repeat what you've heard. Also take the time to explain concepts without being verbose, and ask questions to illicit interaction. In our presentation, the fewer the words we show and say, the better.

What have we done here? We've introduced our customer as the hero in this story by showing someone in a similar situation named John. He looks like a smart and successful professional, just like our customer. He's not unhappy, but he's not yet beaming. He's adequate, just like our prospect. We've described his Ordinary World in three sentences while also raising curiosity and tension. Recall how Joan Johnston opens a scene by using eight techniques. Raising a question and forecasting potential danger are two of them. Our audience is now curious. The final bullet point raises the question of why John might not be protected, and our prospect wants an answer. Is there a bomb under John's table that's about to explode?

So far, to convey our concept, we've used only one graphic and three bullet points. In the next chapter, we'll learn how to use six more bullets to terrify prospects.

CONCLUSIONS

- To tell a good story, we need to focus on how a FROG ACTS.
- We must build trust before we can sell someone swampland in Florida.
- When presenting, use one pic and three bullet points on a slide versus writing a thesis.

FROG ACTS Messaging Framework template

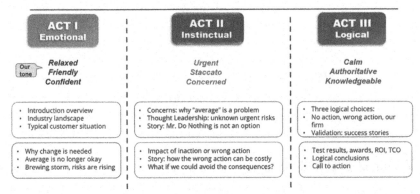

CHAPTER 11
DROWNING

*"The greatest mistake you can make is to be con-
tinually fearing that you'll make one."*
—Elbert Hubbard

ACT IIA: CONCERNED RISKS

I n Act IIa, we should seek to understand our prospect's perceived concerns while also informing him about unknown risks. Our objective is to make him feel uncomfortable. This is the P in SPIN Selling and "Rational Drowning" in *The Challenger Sale*. For the latter, the authors did not discuss neuroscience, so the word "rational" may not be the best choice as we're not yet appealing to the rational brain, or neocortex. "Drowning" is also not the best choice, as we never want to drown our prospects, even metaphorically, but we do want them to be concerned about risks. We want to understand their story while also using stories to initially increase cortisol, which is the chemical in our brain that acts like a yellow light. Stress, anxiety, fear, and concern can increase cortisol. On a temporary basis, we feel uncomfortable, on edge, and have heightened awareness and retention. All this sounds bad, and if maintained long term it can be, but in a short-term situation, it's exactly what we want. Unfortunately, when our prospects feel uncomfortable, so do we.

While engaging with hundreds of recruiting, sales, and marketing professionals across more than two decades, my colleagues and I have noted a common theme. Few want to torture their prospects. It seems counterintuitive to do so while trying to foster a relationship. Yet, as we've learned from the best writers, this is what we *must* do. We all need to channel Diana Gabaldon and inflict some pain on our protagonist. Probing for problems will make our prospect wrinkle their brow and squirm in their seat. This is a necessary evil because if we don't do this, we'll never truly understand who they are, what "keeps them up at night," and how we can help them.

The Challenger Sale authors refer to this as challenging the prospect's beliefs, which requires courage. They recognized this as being easier for some personality types than others, but incorrectly labeled them as *salesperson* types rather than *people* types. They also incorrectly concluded that if you're not a Challenger type, you suck and will never sell anything to anyone. Unless, of course, you pay them huge sums of money to learn how. More than a decade after that book was written, we know from brain science that if you're the type that's conflict-avoidant, helpful, or highly optimistic, challenging anyone can be difficult. However, it's not impossible, and these individuals often become some of the best sales and marketing pros. If the approaches outlined in this chapter make *you* uncomfortable, that's good, as it's how your prospects should also feel.

Dr. Zak and other neuroscientists have discovered that increasing cortisol sharpens our powers of concentration. Again, we're focused more on Aristotle's Pathos techniques and appealing to the instinctual brain. Therefore, we need to employ visual elements and not so much written copy or facts and figures. Says Dr. Garcia-Fresco, "In actuality, your decisions result from the reptilian brain influence. You need to connect to the basic instinctive part of someone's brain before you try to rationalize with people. We all want to believe that we make rational and thoughtful decisions, but reality shows that all of our decisions begin as emotional or instinctual decisions using our reptilian or emotional brains. We then take a second step to rationalize it in our rational brain. This means that our core decision-making relies on our primal instincts and emotions first."

For our presentation, which Act is slide 2? Act II, of course. However, we've divided Act II into two separate segments (a and b), and therefore each slide should represent 25 percent of our story. What part of the brain are we primarily engaging in this act? Instinctually, you should know this. It's the instinctual brain, or reptilian R-complex. Recall how our emotional and instinctual brains are responsible for more than 90 percent of our decision-making. In Act IIa, we're seeking to raise a brain chemical that influences this part of the brain, but do you recall which one?

Cortisol. As noted, it's our brain's "early warning" signal. So what color should we use? Nope, not yellow. Orange is the right answer, or lighter shades of red. For marketers, you don't need to use this color exclusively; just ensure it's predominate and not conflicting alongside dark blues, light greens, etc.

Our visuals should convey concern, warning, problems, and so forth. Our picture on slide 2 should show John with a worried or concerned face and perhaps relevant images in the background, such as an orange warning light or an alert symbol. What about vocal and copy tone? Top writers use a more active tone in Act II to create a faster pace. The train has left the station and it's gaining speed. Sentences and paragraphs become shorter, more compressed. Time becomes its own character, and it's always in short supply. For salespersons, your vocal timbre should have a note of apprehension, as if you're warning a friend about an impending danger. Lean forward slightly in your seat. Do not use too many facts, figures, numbers, or data. For business pros, use short bullet points and active verbs that portray potential risks.

Here's an example:

John had read the latest headlines

Ransomware attacks now devastated firms every ten seconds

Traditional endpoint security had not stopped these attacks

ACT IIB: TENSE OBSTACLES

Now the Wicked Witch of the West had but one eye, yet that was as powerful as a telescope, and could see everywhere. So, as she sat in the door of her castle, she happened to look around and saw Dorothy lying asleep, with her friends all about her. They were a long distance off, but the Wicked Witch was angry to find them in her country; so she blew upon a silver whistle that hung around her neck.

At once there came running to her from all directions a pack of great wolves. They had long legs and fierce eyes and sharp teeth.

"Go to those people," said the Witch, "and tear them to pieces."

"Are you not going to make them your slaves?" asked the leader of the wolves.

"No," she answered, "one is of tin, and one of straw; one is a girl and another a Lion. None of them is fit to work, so you may tear them into small pieces."

"Very well," said the wolf, and he dashed away at full speed, followed by the others.

Even as an adult, decades after originally reading this story, this scene still sends shivers down my spine. This is an example of suspense versus surprise. While Dorothy and her friends lay sleeping, the Wicked Witch sent a deadly pack of wolves to "tear them into small pieces." Dorothy is unaware, but *we* know she is in mortal danger. Because Baum fashioned her as a sympathetic character, we care about her. We don't want her or her friends to be harmed. We desperately want to warn them, but alas, we can't. So all we can do is frantically turn pages and hope they survive. Baum uses tension here to build suspense and drive the story toward the climax.

We can also do this with our prospects or candidates. By using stories, whether told to prospects by salespersons or in written form on a landing page or PDF, we should use tension to build suspense. Here's an example:

> *John had read about other IT executives who ignored the warnings about ransomware and suffered severe consequences. He and his team knew they needed to act quickly and decisively, before it was too late. At the time, John did not know about the REvil ransomware gang. Well funded and staffed by experienced hackers, they were about to strike against dozens of firms around the globe. The REvil gang had spent months preparing, finding gaps in security and using brute force attacks to sneak through "back doors" in unsuspecting firms. They had planted hibernating malware and stealthy root kits on endpoints. With fingers poised above keyboards, they were about to hit "enter" and wreak havoc. The average ransom had skyrocketed past $2 million, and the cost of remediation could be over four times that amount. At the time, John was unaware that his firm had been targeted by the REvil gang, and they were only days away from striking.*

In similar fashion to Baum, we've positioned the REvil ransomware gang as menacing wolves about to attack our hero. Will John act in time to overcome the obstacles and avoid the consequences? Of course he will, but even knowing this does not lessen the suspense or the tension. A few who are reading this may be rolling eyes, believing we're perhaps going a bit over the top here and straying too far from safe and corporate blue. If that's your viewpoint, you're welcome to continue selling, recruiting, or marketing without using stories while your competition "tears you to pieces." Safe is not always safe.

In Act IIb, our goal is to go beyond making our prospect feel uncomfortable by scaring him to death. I exaggerate, but in a great story, we must raise the stakes. After increasing cortisol in Act IIa, our objective in Act IIb is to raise norepinephrine (norep for short) by increasing tension, anxiety, and concern. As we know, norep is essentially noradrenaline, or adrenaline. It skyrockets when we're in danger, being attacked, in fear, or our sports team is about to get their tails kicked.

By increasing our prospect's norep level, we walk a fine line, as we don't want to delve into "fear-based" selling. Instead, we want to employ "risk-based selling." The former might be depicted as "buy my stuff or you're going to die in a car wreck," whereas the latter is "you may be driving toward a cliff and should consider a different road."

The I in Neil Rackham's SPIN Selling stands for "implication." Many sales and marketing professionals either miss or skim over this vital part of the process. Perhaps they hear the prospect utter a problem and immediately deliver a solution. "You have a problem? I can solve it with our silver super stuff!"

The Challenger Sale refers to this step as "Emotional Impact." Again, they did not consider neuroscience or the "impact" this step has on the brain. A more accurate definition might be *instinctual* impact. Most sales methodologies note the importance of raising the stakes, which raises the value of your product or solution. If the impact, implication, or consequences of not properly solving your prospect's problems isn't high enough, the prospect will either have no interest in your solution or will perceive it as worth far less than its cost.

Let's pause for a quick quiz question: Who is your biggest competitor? If you thought of a competitive company name, you are incorrect and must now take a "time-out" with your nose in the corner for at least an hour. No sniveling. Top sales and marketing pros know the correct answer is Mr. Do Nothing. Your prospect is in Kansas. They look around and see a dull, gray, and dusty landscape. They are perhaps bored or unfulfilled, but they are still in an adequate comfort zone. Nothing short of a tornado will move them out of their Ordinary World. Doing nothing takes no effort, conjures no fear, and is perceived as a safe choice. Our job is to educate our prospect and help them see how doing nothing is not safe and carries far more risk than perceived. We must appeal to their instinctual brain and help them see the impact or implication of making no choice, or making the wrong choice. This is best done with a story.

Recall in our opening story how Linda told John a customer horror story?

As noted, Linda and her colleague also used the element of time to heighten the tension, stakes, and impact. During our journey through Acts IIa and b, we need to go back and forth across the tension line while increasing the stakes. We can do this by asking questions, which will help the prospect feel more in control. Then, we should challenge his or her beliefs with thought-provoking information and danger-filled stories that warn of serious consequences for inaction or wrong action. This will create a ying-yang effect similar to a roller-coaster ride. We feel fine when the coaster is slowly climbing, then we cling to our seat belts with fear when we're propelled toward the rapid decline.

On the best rides, there's also an unexpected turn that surprises us.

Once we've deftly used the element of suspense to raise tension and stakes, we should also use surprise toward the end of Act IIb to propel our story toward the climactic finish. Recall how the Wicked Witch, right before she turned over the sand-filled hourglass, told Dorothy that her slippers were magical and could not be removed while she was still alive? We can also use the element of surprise in stories we impart to prospects.

To increase suspense and lay the foundation for surprise in our presentation, our vocal tone should become even more concerned and faster. Use active verbs and shorter sentences, paragraphs, and chapters. Lean forward even more in your seat. Again, refrain from using graphs, facts, figures, and numbers. Instead, continue to use short bullet points. For our graphics, our hero should invoke a pose depicting a response to a negative event, such as a hand to his forehead, a frown, his head down, etc. Our predominate color should be red, perhaps tinged with orange.

The hero can be wearing black, but not lighter colors such as green, yellow, or blue. Example bullet points might be:

Attackers exploited a gap in John's security

The firm's endpoint security failed to prevent the breach

They were told to pay the ransom or risk severe brand damage

The surprise here is subtle but still present. John thought his firm was protected but was surprised to discover they were not, and the consequences were severe. The surprise also sets up the climax to our story. How will John deal with this attack and overcome the obstacles? Will our hero prevail? Recall that the climactic peak can occur at the end of Act IIb or beginning of Act III. For our presentation, we'll use the latter as we help our terrified prospect find his way back home in Act III.

CONCLUSIONS

- In Act II, we should scare the crap out of people. Or at least ensure they're concerned.
- Our biggest competitor is Mr. Do Nothing, who's a mean guy with small ears.
- We should increase tension to increase the stakes to increase our wallets.

CHAPTER 12
NO PLACE LIKE HOME

*"It's a funny thing coming home. Nothing changes.
Everything looks the same, feels the same, even smells
the same. You realized what's changed is you."*
—F. Scott Fitzgerald

ACT III: SATISFIED GAINS

n Act IIb, we told a story that portrays our prospect's worst nightmare. In doing so, we essentially scared him to death, which was our objective. We raised cortisol and then norepinephrine. With his adrenaline surging, our prospect was uncomfortable. Again, this is a difficult thing to do for many, as it's contrary to our desire to build a relationship. Also again, it is a necessary evil, but once accomplished, we can offer hope.

While telling a story about a customer, Linda portrayed someone faced with similar concerns and risks as her prospect. For the story's climax, prior to showing the next slide in the presentation, Linda might say to her prospect, "Joe at XYZ Company had little time to act. Files had been encrypted, systems were down, and productivity had ground to a halt. If he could not immediately remove the damage caused by the ransomware, his firm would likely pay millions in ransom and remediation costs. The downtime costs and brand damage could also be devastating. What John needed was a miracle."

Linda can then display the Act III slide. "Fortunately, John found that miracle. He'd recently installed a way to turn back the clock with ransomware rollback technology. With a few mouse clicks, he unwound the damage and returned all the encrypted files to a prior state before the attack. This saved the company millions."

In Act III, we need to hit the brakes. We need to primarily employ Aristotle's Logos techniques by slowing down, becoming more analytical and authoritative, and appealing to our prospect's logical brain so they can feel satisfied with the decision they're about to make and gains they're about to receive. We can do this by increasing GABA and serotonin levels, as this has a calming effect on the mind, which can help make our prospects more receptive to logical information.

GABA is the antithesis of norepinephrine and cortisol and is a natural chemical in our brain that helps us chill. It can be found in many supplements designed for mood regulation and stress relief. Serotonin, as we know, is a neurotransmitter that also helps with mood, as well as staying positive, cheerful, and smiling. When our brains are sufficiently pumping out GABA and/or serotonin, we are usually more relaxed and therefore more receptive to rational information.

Studies have shown that positive visualization can increase serotonin levels in the brain, and this happens in spades when we become engrossed in an engaging story. For example, when we read a great mystery novel, after we've pulled our hearts out of our throats during the climax, we're amazed at how the protagonist catches the killer in Act III by logically forming a picture from all the disjointed clues. Likewise, in the Act III return phase of the Hero's Journey, we help our prospects visualize the right logical choice so they can return with the "magic elixir" of wisdom and impart that gift to their firm. As Joseph Campbell says, "The hero is the champion of things becoming, not of things become."

As we know, our brains prefer information delivered in threes. There's a reason why most HGTV shows, wherein couples are looking for a new home, show only three property choices. Sure, the buyers probably saw thirty homes, but we viewers only see the final three because that's the optimal number for "choosing." Adept marketers know this intuitively, which is why they often display only three choices on a website. While attempting to close prospects in Act III, we're wise to appeal to their analytical brains by giving them only three logical choices.

Choice number one: Mr. Do Nothing. Since this guy is your biggest competitor, make him the first choice. Because we've done such an excellent job of covering the consequences of inaction in Act IIb, we can now analytically show why this is a bad decision. We can use numbers, graphs, charts, and ROI data to explain this. For our presentation example, the Act III slide should show our hero smiling and calm. He should look triumphant. After all, he just slayed the Wicked Witch of the West. He should be wearing deep blue or similar colors, and the predominate background colors should be blue, indigo, and/or violet. Our vocal tone should be calm and authoritative. We should use a slower pace and display more graphs, charts, data, and numbers. Our three bullet examples might be:

1. **Choice #1: John did nothing and his firm paid $4M in ransom and damages.**
2. **Choice #2: John chose an inferior solution that could not unwind the damage.**
3. **Choice #3: John avoided all costs by deploying a solution with ransomware rollback.**

While unveiling each bullet one at a time, Linda might say, "John, we explored problems related to believing typical security solutions are adequate enough to prevent ransomware. As we recall, the average ransom now exceeds $2 million, but the cost of cleaning up the mess can be at least twice that. Given these serious consequences, and given that most solutions don't achieve better than 80 percent prevention, ignoring this issue is obviously not an option, right?"

Below Choice #1 (prior to showing the other two choices), Linda can display a graph, chart, and numbers, such as $4M. When she clicks to show Choice #2, the number changes to, say, $2M, indicating that an inferior choice is better but might only reduce the damage by 50 percent. As she clicks again to display Choice #3, the number changes to $0. The gain, obviously, is measured in millions.

During Act III, there is always "that guy" who has to be cantankerous and will argue with the numbers displayed, so be sure to use figures that are conservative and validated by credible sources. Caution here: we don't want to denigrate specific competitors with a smug snarl or pompous superiority stance, and we don't want to make our prospect feel like an idiot for choosing a crappy solution (even if he is one). We *can* use facts and figures from reliable sources that throw spears at competitors, but we should do this without displaying emotion. We're simply appealing to our prospect's logical brain by presenting facts derived by others. The data should be indisputable, such as analyst reports, test results, and independent studies. It's not *us* saying this about the other guys, it's *them*.

If our prospect dismisses or disputes the data, don't argue with them. The best way to handle objections is to turn them into questions and answer the questions. For example, if John says, "With an 80 percent prevention rate, my risk is still only 20 percent. I think I can live with that." Linda might say, "John, I believe the question you're asking is why isn't 80 percent good enough? Why should you be concerned about only 20 percent? The answer is, as you recall, a ransomware attack now occurs every ten seconds, and your industry is one of the most prone to attack. Also as we discussed, every leading industry analyst now says it's no longer a matter of *if* but *when* you will be attacked. Do you recall the story I presented? That firm also thought 80 percent was high enough…"

No, this will not work in every case. John may remain unconvinced, and you may need to gently continue guiding. At some point, you may hit a wall and be forced to walk away. Not every prospect will buy. However, you've at least planted seeds that may take time to grow. Your prospect may need to discuss this with others, review more information, or take more time to process what he's learned. Just because he doesn't immediately jump on a trampoline while waving a PO in your face does not mean he's a lost cause. We've all heard the age-old adage that "the sale begins when the prospect says no."

When we close our discussion with someone in Act III, they should feel satisfied with the potential gains, as if they've just closed the cover on a great book. Memorable and impactful stories are ones that leave us with mixed emotions. We're delighted by the masterful ending, but sad the story is over. With most prospects, we likely won't close them in the first meeting—as in we got a PO—but we should close them on the next step in the journey by clearly outlining the gains of working together as a team.

Think of this as a series of books. Each one can stand on its own, but the overall story continues. George Lucas brought us the *Star Wars* movie series. He started in the middle with *Episode IV—A New Hope*, where he introduced us to the hero, Luke Skywalker. When this movie ends, we are satisfied, as many foes were vanquished, but the ultimate antagonist is still out there and still a threat. We know there's another saga coming, and we await its arrival with anticipation. When we "close" a prospect in most business-to-business (B2B) situations, and sometimes in business-to-consumer (B2C) scenarios, we rarely finalize a transaction in the first engagement or meeting. Therefore, as noted, we're usually not closing for a PO but rather next steps. We're concluding this episode and laying the foundation for the next one. Once we've delivered "a new hope" to our prospect, we want to preview and schedule the next episode. We want to let them know what to expect when "the empire strikes back," and when it will be released. We also want to sell them a ticket.

In the first "book of business" with our prospect, our end goal may be to move forward by "selling them a ticket" to a subsequent meeting, perhaps with others on the team or with those involved in the decision-making process. Many sales and marketing professionals agree there are three main objectives to every close: agreement, appointment, and agenda.

Our first objective is to ensure we and our prospect are in agreement. We should review what we've discussed and agree on the primary concerns and consequences. We should also agree on the optimal logical choice to prevent those consequences. We should then agree on a date and time—even if a placeholder—for an appointment to meet again to dive deeper into that logical choice. We should agree on who will attend that meeting, from both organizations, and three main objectives—our agenda. Yes, this is different from an agenda in the beginning of a presentation, as it refers to the goals we want to accomplish in our next meeting.

Once we've completed the above, we should hand our prospect a small bag with toothpaste and a toothbrush and remind them to floss. Or…we should leave them with an ARC like Linda did in our opening story. This ARC, as we recall, stands for attainable results chart. This simple but powerful chart will help our prospect prepare for our next meeting. It should not include details about our solution, and our vendor name or information should be subtle. The ARC should include information and illustrative graphics or icons to depict a before and after scenario. Below again is the one Linda gave to John:

ARC:

FROM: *Cloud software encryption that exposes the company to security risks*

TO: *Hardware encryption cloud solution that eliminates security risks*

WHY: *To ensure compliance with state bills and mitigate fines and lawsuits*

HOW: *Fast, simple, painless migration*

WHAT: *Affordable hardware encryption cloud solution with a nine-month ROI*

Providing an ARC will help ensure our prospect is armed with important and memorable morsels of information he or she can impart to others who will also need to be sold. Remember, most of the sale is done "offline" after you've left the building or Zoom call. Your prospect needs to become an evangelist who can easily and deftly repeat what she's learned. She needs to be ready and able to deliver the "magic elixir" of knowledge she's received to others who still dwell in the Ordinary World. To ensure retention and impact, the magic elixir—the *gains*—should leverage Aristotle's Persuasion Model and appeal to the emotional, instinctual, and logical brain.

Now that you're a storytelling expert, you may have surmised the ARC's double entendre. It also stands for the character arc found in every great story. The Hero's Journey is often depicted as an arc. Visualize a half-circle arc spanning from scene one in Act I to the final scene in Act III. Our hero should transition from where they were to what they want to be. Dorothy went from bored, unfulfilled, and unchallenged in her dull Ordinary World to happy and wise and back home again after being tested. She completed her journey and brought back the magic elixir of truth. Our prospect has the opportunity to make a similar journey, and the ARC shows them how to do this. The ARC also provides our prospect with a cheat sheet to impart our value props to others in the firm who need to be persuaded.

While our new evangelist is busy selling on our behalf, we can relax on our yacht in Monaco while preparing our slide deck and script for the next meeting. On the other side of the world, marketing can diligently start working on creating more success stories to help persuade customers to avoid choosing the dark side.

CONCLUSIONS

- In Act III, we should calm people down with Zoloft (GABA also works).
- We should give prospects a toothbrush and an ARC (contrasting story arc).
- Get an agreement, appointment, and agenda…or…get another job.

CHAPTER 13

THREE CHOICES

"A plethora of options creates a poverty of commitment."
—Shane Parrish

S tar Wars: The Empire Strikes Back did not begin with Act III. Even though most who watched this film knew the characters and much about the galaxy they inhabited, George Lucas started again with Act I. We were reintroduced to this world, and the motivations and desires of our hero and villain were reignited. The same approach is required for our second and subsequent prospect meetings. We need to start over with Act I each time we meet. We need to again ask about our prospect's Ordinary World and understand if anything has changed. Have they met with other peers or decision-makers to review the ARC or other aspects of our last discussion? Have they had any incidents, or do they have additional questions? Have they reviewed the information we gave them? Wassup in Kansas these days?

We can then remind them about the flying monkeys or wolf packs they might face in Act II, and about the three logical choices we analyzed in Act III. The last we spoke, Mr. Prospect, we agreed that Choice #3, our stuff, was the most logical one and here again is why. Are we still in agreement? If not, why not? If not, you obviously need to be tortured on the rack again so let's go back to Act II and hang out for a while.

We may also need to whip out more success stories to help them move past their fear of indecision or wrong decision. Remember, in many cases, our prospect's career and reputation may be on the line. They may be hesitant to risk either, and for some individuals, going with Mr. Do Nothing seems safer. They don't want to rock the boat, especially if they're sailing on a rickety old one, or Captain Bligh is at the helm. They may need frequent nudging and reminding that *safe is not always safe*.

Once we've returned to Act III, as we know, sharing success stories can be one of the most powerful ways to help prospects or candidates move beyond their fear. They can become encouraged by the courage of others who took a risk with your firm and succeeded. Across two decades of consulting for some of the world's largest and most successful sales teams, the number one sales enablement request has always been "more success stories." Coincidentally, across thousands of prospect and customer calls—whether in person, on the phone, or on Zoom—prospects also place a high value on these assets. They want assurances that a solution has worked well for others in similar situations. Marketers should take note here. Some of your most important assets are success stories. Please don't call them "case studies." They are not cases, and they are not studies. Using that term will make you sound like a college professor with a superiority complex. Also, these should be written as *stories*. They should have a hero (the customer) and follow the three-act play format.

I've personally written quite a few success stories for firms like Booz Allen Hamilton, Cisco, HP, Visa, and Fortinet—the world's largest security technology firm. In some cases, many of their previous "case studies" had received less than favorable marks from both the sales team and prospects. Once written using proper storytelling techniques, they received the highest praise from both. Success stories can and should be one of the most important weapons in your arsenal, and one of the most important sections within these stories is Act IIb, which sets up Act III. This part is frequently left out of most success stories because marketers are loathe to discuss the dismal consequences faced by prospects. It's also difficult to get your customers to talk about failures with other solutions, as doing so may reflect badly on them and their firm. Getting customers to reveal a few "dirty little secrets" does take practice and diplomacy, but it can be done. One trick I've used is to employ hypothetical situations or "other firm" examples. You might say, "John had read about other IT executives who ignored similar issues and suffered severe consequences. He and his team knew they needed to act quickly and decisively, before it was too late."

Another mistake many marketers make is to expend 90 percent of the copy on their solutions. Act III is an important part of any success story, but it should represent only 25 percent of the document. Most success stories spend about 5 percent of the copy on a few hypothetical industry problems (Act I), perhaps by quoting an analyst or expert, and then another 10 percent of the story on a few typical customer concerns (Act II). The rest of the copy then focuses on the vendor's solutions (Act III). This makes the vendor the hero instead of the customer while appealing mostly to the logical brain. When we write a success story, it should be a story, not an advertisement.

Let's explore a few secrets about how to use proper storytelling techniques in written documents, including success stories, and how to impart this information to prospects, candidates, or customers. We'll start by examining a less effective approach…

Ineffective "Push Model" Messaging

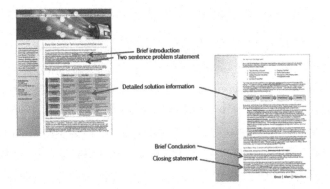

As we can see in the example above, business assets are often veiled ads and are therefore less effective. They use a "push" messaging technique, which essentially pushes information onto the reader. They read more like a data sheet than a story. As we can see, the authors of this document spent too little time in Act I or II and almost all their time in Act III. Aristotle would be sadly disappointed while wringing his tunic and shaking his ancient head. Solving this dilemma requires using a cube. A messaging cube, not a Rubik's cube.

3-Act Storytelling Messaging Cube

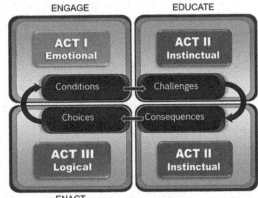

By the way, this cube can be used for virtually any written document from a success story to a solution brief, white paper, blog, ebook, article, email, job description, LinkedIn message, or sales script. This will help you employ a three-act play story format while also aligning with Aristotle's Persuasion Model and popular sales frameworks. Your written documents will be smooth, captivating, and tantalizing. Readers will sing praises about your writing prowess and throw roses at your feet. Or, they will just buy your stuff, which is even better.

There are four parts to the messaging cube, just as there are four parts to the three-act play (Acts I, IIa, IIb, III). Starting from the upper left and progressing clockwise, the cube uses our two acronyms: FROG ACTS. As we know, FROG is related to *our* actions and ACTS to the *prospect's* reactions. Again, FROG stands for Focus, Risks, Obstacles, and Gains, which are the actions we should take in order to illicit the prospect's ACTS reactions. ACTS stands for Adequate, Concerned, Tense, and Satisfied, which describes how the prospect *feels* after reacting to our FROG sales, recruiting, or marketing approach.

Beginning with Act I, we should focus on our prospect's adequate Ordinary World. In writing our document, we can begin with an introductory statement—what our document is about—followed by statements and/or questions related to our protagonist's situation. An example might be:

> "Recent headlines are replete with news about escalating ransomware threats. Attacks have become more frequent and sophisticated, bypassing even the best defenses. Given increases in remote or hybrid work, endpoints—including PCs, notebooks, and mobile phones—have become weaker links in your security chain…"

This example uses the Socrates deductive reasoning approach by stating indisputable facts (without throwing out too many numbers) that can only illicit an affirmative nod by our audience. Within our first few paragraphs, we're getting our prospect to frequently say "yes, I agree with this industry situation." We also want to deliver unique and perhaps unknown information to pique interest. We might say something like...

> "To avoid detection, attackers now employ obfuscated malware, root kits, and stealth techniques that are often missed by traditional endpoint security solutions. Once inside the gates of your castle, these malicious threats may lay dormant for days or weeks before moving laterally across your network to infect multiple systems. Even if detected on one machine, they may be difficult to eradicate, as each instance can generate a hundred or more artifacts..."

Since we began our teaching session with indisputable and likely known facts that should spur silent "yes, I agree" responses from the reader, we can now layer unknown and interesting information atop these facts that will keep the prospect in agreement mode and help move them beyond feeling adequate in their Ordinary World.

Again, the purpose of Act I is to let the prospect know that we know they are the hero of the story, we are the wise mentor in their story, and their Ordinary World sucks. It's not as adequate as they may have perceived, and it's time to move on. We need to nudge or even thrust them into Act II. As we know, Act I should be about 25 percent of our document.

Moving clockwise on the cube, in Act IIa we discuss risks to help our prospect feel concern. Here we turn up the heat and boil the frog's water to make them feel uncomfortable. We use stories within our story to portray what others are concerned about and the consequences of inaction or wrong action. We then move to Act III, where we increase the tension at the story's climax before we deliver our three logical choices: Mr. (or Ms.) Do Nothing, Mr. (or Ms.) Deficient, and Mr. (or Ms.) Perfect (us). Here we can deliver our speeds and feeds, facts and figures, return on investment, and total cost of ownership data, and then our call to action.

3-Act Storytelling messaging example

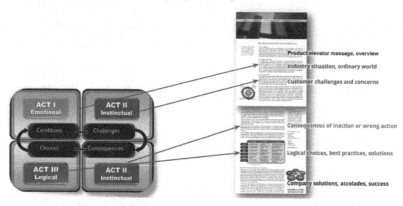

Let's now see how to use our messaging cube to create a messaging guide, which should be the foundation for everything we write, including success stories.

CONCLUSIONS

- We should not be pushy, we should be "pulley."
- We should offer three logical choices; one should not be Guido with a baseball bat.
- The three choices are Mr. Do Nothing, Mr. Deficient, and Mr. Perfect—us!

CHAPTER 14
GUIDE ME

Messaging framework structure

Alignment with Sales Methodologies, Persuasion Model, Storytelling Approach

Sales Methodologies:
- Alignment with sales methodology training (e.g; Sandler, SPIN, Miller Heiman, Challenger, etc.) to ensure sales team adoption.

Persuasion Model:
- Alignment with the proven Aristotle Persuasion Model to ensure resonance across a wide universe of personas.

Storytelling Approach:
- Alignment with the standard 3-Act Play, proven to enhance retention by 1400% and trust by 300%.

Graphic created by the author

"What we've got here is failure to communicate."
—Captain's speech in the movie *Cool Hand Luke*

A messaging guide should use a framework that aligns sales methodologies (Miller Heiman, Sandler, Challenger, etc.) with Aristotle's Persuasion Model and the three-act play storytelling approach. It should be used to form the foundation for every type of message used by an organization, including web pages, blogs, solution briefs, presentations, press releases, job descriptions, and success stories. As noted earlier, messaging guide details are beyond the scope of this book, but you can visit RemotelyMe.com/consulting to download a messaging guide framework.

Below are a few examples of the types of collateral that can be created using a messaging guide that contains all three of the above elements.

This is an example of an actual published success story I wrote that uses the FROG ACTS storytelling framework to capture a prospect's attention and influence their decision. This was a story about a reseller, written for one of the world's largest tech firms and their biggest distributor. I've changed only the names of the people and companies.

Headline

Providing Superior Managed Services to Clients with Tech Networks Security Solutions and Services

Introduction

Ray Bayon is the president and founder of AB Networks, a managed services provider (MSP) in the Southeast. AB assists small and medium businesses by providing services and solutions to meet their information technology (IT) and security needs. In 2018, Ray started his business by himself in a small eighty-square-foot office with no employees. Over the next several years, by offering best-in-class expertise and industry-leading products, Ray leveraged his professional experience in electronics medical records and other industries to grow the firm to twenty-five employees. He has since invested in a 30,000-square-foot building and more technology infrastructure to service clients.

"Our clients rely on us to deliver superb IT and security services, expertise, and solutions," says Ray. "We now offer a variety of managed and project services, including remote monitoring to detect and remediate vulnerabilities and threats."

The above is Act I, wherein we introduce the hero, Ray, and create a sympathetic character by showcasing his expertise and how he worked hard to build a successful business from scratch.

The Challenge

AB had been using a well-known security vendor to provide service offerings but became concerned about inconsistencies with services and pricing. "We rely on commitments from our vendors to properly service our clients," says Ray. "We also need to maintain a technology leadership position, so it's vital that our vendors do the same and do not fall behind technically."

Ray and the dedicated team at AB had worked hard over several years to help their clients solve a host of problems, including downtime due to underpowered network switches with limited feature sets, security vulnerabilities against unknown zero-day malware, and vulnerable remote endpoints. They built a strong industry reputation and a growing list of satisfied clients. Given escalations in cybersecurity threats, exacerbated by a more remote working environment, Ray did not want to risk his business, or his client's businesses, on inadequate solutions or vendors.

"We selected SecNet, as they offer industry-leading security technology," says Ray. "The SecNet security suite includes Next-Generation Firewalls (NGFWs) and bulletproof network security, as well as an affordable hardware-as-a-service model that's attractive to our clients."

The above is Act II, where we outline Ray's challenges and concerns and build toward the climax. Now that we, as readers, have learned that Ray worked so hard to build his business, we also don't want to see him risk everything on inadequate solutions or vendors.

The Solution

SecNet introduced AB to one of their leading distributors, Tech Networks, as they offer excellent support, value-added services, and superior expertise. Tech Networks also provided Ray's team with product training and deployment assistance.

"We were impressed with Tech Network's knowledge, responsiveness, and training," says Ray. "Our clients have been very satisfied with SecNet solutions, including NGFWs, network switches, and secure wireless access points. The icing on the cake is SecNet's hardware-as-a-service model that allows us to offer attractive monthly service charges bundled with our managed services."

The Results

Ray estimates that SecNet's solutions, combined with services and support from Tech Networks, has reduced AB's costs to manage clients and deploy solutions in half.

"Tech Networks provided excellent training and expertise to help us implement SecNet's products," says Ray. "SecNet's superior efficiency and speed has allowed us to deploy lower cost models that offer the same or better performance as compared to more expensive competitive solutions. This has allowed us to improve our margins while lowering client costs. We can use more automated scripts rather than manual processes, which lowers personnel costs and facilitates better scalability."

Given fast response times from a team of knowledgeable experts, AB has derived significant benefits from its relationship with Tech Networks. "They are easy to work with, friendly, and sharp," says Ryan. "They keep their commitments and ensure our working relationship is seamless and smooth. That allows us to ensure that our clients are thrilled with our service and solution offerings."

AB has continued to expand its business and enhance its industry reputation by offering clients industry-leading security solutions from SecNet coupled with outstanding distribution services from Tech Networks.

In Act III, we show how the wise mentor, Tech Networks, used SecNet solutions to help Ray bring home the magic elixir and expand his business. Why is a proper storytelling structure important? Because readers will be less likely to believe Ray when he raves about these vendors if he had not first struggled through Act I and Act II. What makes Ray a trustable and believable character if he has not faced adversity? Would you believe your neighbor when he recommends an auto mechanic if he'd only had an occasional oil change and not a serious problem solved by that mechanic? Perhaps not. This illustrates the power of a story in a success story. It does not have to be sappy or over the top and can still take a polished "business blue" approach while impacting an audience with a proper storytelling structure. Again, these vendors are among the largest and most successful security firms in the world. This success story received very high marks from their sales and marketing teams, and from those who downloaded and read the document.

SALES SCRIPT

The following is an example of a sales script "door opener" delivered as an email, LinkedIn Message, or SalesLoft cadence:

Act I: Adequate Focus

Hi John, I'm interested in your expert opinion about endpoint security solutions that are failing to stop ransomware attacks, now occurring every ten seconds. I'm offering a twenty-five-dollar gift card for twenty-five minutes of your time to learn how your team is preventing these attacks to avoid brand damage and millions in remediation costs.

Act IIa: Concerned Risks

One of our customers, the IT director for XYZ Medical Center, had serious concerns about attackers gaining access to sensitive patient data on thin clients. Like most firms, they had limited resources, budget, and time. They were also using a less than adequate solution.

Act IIb: Tense Obstacles

The IT director did not feel safe trusting his data to traditional endpoint protection solutions, as these were obviously failing. With the average ransom exceeding two million, and remediation costs at four million, one breach could have been devastating.

Act III: Satisfied Gains

The IT director needed an economical, effective, and elegant solution to prevent attacks before they caused damage. They found something that easily integrates with their current solution and uses a unique new technology, which leading analysts like Gartner say is a game changer.

CTA

Again, I'm offering a gift card for a few minutes of your time to hear your expert opinion about endpoint security. Please CLICK HERE to schedule our call.

As noted, the above follows our storytelling framework to deliver a brief but compelling message, seeking the expert opinion of our prospect. Typical sales scripts sound like sales scripts, which are far less effective. Every prospect receives these, and most get deleted because they sound like sales scripts. "Hi John, you know, I'm just touching base and I'd be sooooo grateful for thirty seconds of your time so I can sell you something."

Most prospects love to talk about themselves and show off their knowledge. When you send them an invite to do so, you'll receive more responses. Many marketers shun incentives such as gift cards, saying they shouldn't have to offer a gift (because they're stuff is so wicked cool) and they don't want prospects showing up only for an incentive. Sorry, folks, I have to roll my eyes at this type of self-centered attitude.

Sales teams often call a prospect meeting an "at bat." You can't hit the ball or win a game if you never get any at bats. Having worked with dozens of clients where my teams and I scheduled and completed thousands of these types of calls, we found less than 3 percent show up only for an incentive. We're typically scheduling calls with successful executives who don't need a gift card. However, they receive dozens of invites a week from sales reps who are "just touching base." They rarely respond to these. What they may respond to is an opportunity to show off their knowledge about a topic that interests them. The gift card is a consolation prize—likely given to their kids—in case the meeting turns out to be a dud sales call.

There are a few other tricks to note in this sales script example—especially if it's an email. Don't use dollar signs, and spell out the numbers to avoid getting blocked by spam filters. Also, don't tell them anything about your solution. Only provide a brief hint about the benefits found by one of your customers. This creates curiosity, which will improve response rates.

Other items to note in this script: there are two opinions offered here, and they are not ours. One is a satisfied customer; the other is an independent expert (analyst). Recall, we are striving for "yes" responses from our prospects. In essence, we're saying, "You do trust the opinions of a respected medical facility and leading analyst, right?"

Finally, our call to action isn't for a sales call. It's also not really for a gift card. Again, this is only the consolation prize. Our CTA offers our prospects the opportunity to show us how smart they are about a topic of interest. How can they possibly refuse?

The above are a few examples of how we might use storytelling to capture prospect attention and drive high response rates. Now we'll learn how to speak Martian.

CONCLUSIONS

- A messaging guide is like a road map, which, of course, most guys refuse to use.
- The hero of a success story is not us, it's the dude or dudette we're engaging with.
- Stop touching base, unless you're a baseball player making millions.

CHAPTER 15
TAILORING

*"All right everyone, line up alphabetically
according to your height."*
—Casey Stengel

T he Duarte VisualStories workshop teaches us to establish a common ground using shared experiences and goals. Good advice, but like most sales and marketing frameworks, they assume that "one size fits all." In the book *Men Are from Mars, Women Are from Venus* by John Gray, PhD, we learn how to navigate around different communication styles. It's how we're wired. When someone asks if we're an introvert or an extrovert, most of us don't bat an eye. We offer an immediate answer. A few of us straddle the fence, but if we're honest, we tend to lean one way or the other most often.

In this chapter, we'll delve into the true meaning of account-based marketing (ABM), and most importantly, account-based selling (ABS), not to be confused with an automatic braking system. Most marketing pros I've met believe ABM is only about creating different emails for different personas—as in one for decision-makers and one for influencers, or for different vertical markets. Most sales pros don't employ ABS at all, other than wherein marketing provides different customer email cadences based on personas. Recruiters can learn a few lessons from these sales pros because, after all, recruiting is actually selling, right?

I won't bore you with all the logical data supporting the benefits of personalizing messaging and content for various buyers, as the benefits are obvious. What's important, however, is *how* we personalize. It's less about the role a prospect plays and far more about their communication preferences. Are they more logical and prefer lots of detail, facts, and figures? Are they more emotional and resonate best with smiles, relationships, or making their life easier? Or are they more instinctual and want a synopsis with bullet points and the proverbial bottom line? Do they speak Venutian or Martian?

The best sales pros intuitively adjust their communication styles to their prospect's preferences. I learned this valuable lesson the hard way years ago. While serving as a sales and marketing VP at a start-up, I scheduled a meeting with a decision-maker at a Fortune 500 firm. Our company's chief technology officer came with me, and we decided to grab lunch prior to the meeting. While our CTO was brilliant, he was also a bit unkempt and dressed as if he were a lumberjack rather than a company executive. During lunch, he dribbled half his meal all over his shirt. Orange, red, and green stains streaked from under his chin down to his navel. It looked like Walt Disney had power puked on the guy. I cringed. I was certain that our prospect would take one look and usher us out the door.

Filled with trepidation, I drove to the site, where we signed in and waited in the lobby. All the while, our smiling CTO remained oblivious to how he looked. Our prospect strode into the lobby, and I raised an eyebrow. The man was a bit disheveled and wore a lumberjack shirt, which was covered with food stains. Our CTO stood, smiled, and extended a hand. The prospect took one look at the CTO's shirt and grinned. Instant connection. From then on, the two conversed as if long lost brothers, while I stood on the sideline and scratched my head. Then a light bulb came on.

The cardinal sin of sales and marketing is to assume that our prospects like what we like. Just because we think an image or logo or ad or whatever looks great to us does not mean our customers will agree. That's why we do what experts call receptivity factor market research, which is a fancy way of saying we ask target customers what they like. As noted, the most successful pros adjust their communication styles to fit their prospects. This is what *The Challenger Sale* refers to as "tailoring." However, they don't quite approach this correctly. They start with "teaching" and then move to "tailoring." We should tailor first so we can adjust *how* we teach *whom*. To discern how best to approach John, we must first get to know John. *The Challenger Sale* also recommends "old school" approaches to tailoring rather than more modern behavioral or neuroscience-based methods.

My sister, Pam, has a master's degree in educational science and was a teacher for thirty years. One of her daughters is a school principal, and one of my daughters is a teacher. Many teachers now use an educational framework called 4MAT that "tailors" lesson plan formats to learning types, which is akin to personality types. We'll examine a new framework in a later chapter that transcends 4MAT, but for now let's agree it's best to tailor our approach to different communication preferences so we can teach them something. The best way to discern someone's preferences is by asking questions and listening to them communicate, but we must first understand the differences between three primary communication styles.

We learned there are nine distinct types of salespersons because modern neuroscience validates what the ancients knew eons ago: there are nine different personality types. Actually, eighteen if we account for introversion and extroversion. If there are different types of salespersons, then obviously, there are different types of buyers that fall within those same categories.

An article in *Psychology Today* states that around 20 percent of the population is likely more emotionally sensitive in nature (Bergland, 2015). They're the ones who cry at movies. The article cites findings from University of British Columbia and Cornell University neuroscientists who discovered that human genes may influence how sensitive certain people are to emotional information.

In other words, some people may be genetically wired to be more emotional as compared to the average human being. If you cry at sad movies, perhaps your genes are too tight. Okay, bad joke. However, experts did discover that some people have a genetic variation called ADRA2b, which influences the norepinephrine neurotransmitter in our brains (Todd et al., 2015). This variation is linked to heightened activity in certain brain areas that can trigger intense emotional sensitivity and responses.

To summarize, neuroscientists from two respected universities proffered research indicating that a percentage of the human population is genetically wired to be more emotional, which may be directly related to levels of brain norepinephrine. Furthermore, this research shows how the norepinephrine pathways connect directly to the hippocampus and amygdala, which are located in the limbic system. We learned earlier that this is the emotional part of our brain. Did a loud bell just ring?

Adam Anderson, professor of human development at Cornell University and senior author of the study, stated that emotions aren't just about how someone feels about the world but also how a person's brain influences perception. Human genes can influence how a person visualizes negative and positive aspects in their environment.

The American Psychological Association defines personality as the differences in characteristic patterns of thinking, feeling, and behaving. Based on this premise, it appears that norepinephrine influences human personalities and the levels of this neurotransmitter are genetically predisposed. This research study, and many others, infer that there is reciprocal activity between norepinephrine and serotonergic and dopaminergic systems, which are fancy words for serotonin and dopamine production, respectively.

Based on this recent research, it appears that neuroscience, and more specifically the balance between three primary neurotransmitters, may be directly linked to differences in our personalities. If so, how do these profiles relate to the ancient enneagram or more modern frameworks such as the OPQ32? Also, how can business professionals leverage this knowledge to get someone to jump up and down on a trampoline while waving a PO?

As previously noted, many experts agree that neurotransmitters and chemicals modulate brain activity in predictable patterns and influence how we act and interact with others. The three neurotransmitters more involved with personalities are dopamine, serotonin, and norepinephrine (Thomas, 2016, pp. 173–178).

As we know, dopamine is a basic modulator of attention, motivation, pain, and pleasure and regulates how we *behave*. Serotonin modulates obsession, compulsions, and psychological well-being and regulates how we *feel*. Norepinephrine is involved with focused thinking, mental activity, alertness, and energy and regulates how we *think*. Each neurotransmitter's production, or level, is either high, medium, or low. Apparent levels can also be determined by the length of a neurotransmitter's pathway in the brain. This is like a hose used to fill your garden with water. A longer, narrower hose will bring in less water, and vice versa. Based on these brain dynamics, our profiles are divided into three groups: logical, emotional, and instinctual. Hopefully, another loud bell just rang?

Color Spectrum impact on messaging

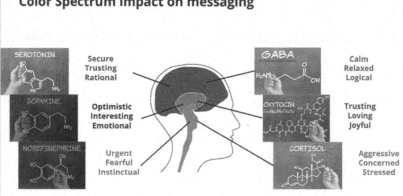

SEROTONIN — Secure / Trusting / Rational

GABA — Calm / Relaxed / Logical

DOPAMINE — Optimistic / Interesting / Emotional

OXYTOCIN — Trusting / Loving / Joyful

NOREPINEPHRINE — Urgent / Fearful / Instinctual

CORTISOL — Aggressive / Concerned / Stressed

NEUROSCIENCE-BASED PERSONALITY PROFILING

Two renowned experts interviewed for this book, Dr. Eric S. Schulze and Dr. Tina Thomas, discovered that the enneagram's observational science can be explained by genetically determined high, medium, or low levels of dopamine, serotonin, and norepinephrine.

The ancient enneagram's nine types are divided into three distinct groups of three personality types each. The three groups, or triads, can be defined as "head types" (more logical), "heart types" (more emotional), and "gut types" (more instinctual). Schulze and Thomas discovered that the thinking group types appear to have higher levels of norepinephrine activity and are generally mentally active. The instinctual types have lower norepinephrine activity, and the heart types have medium activity.

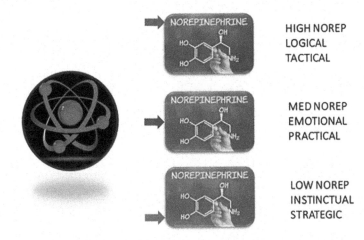

Schulze and Thomas found that norepinephrine regulates how quickly and how often a person thinks and solves problems. Thomas reports that "people who have a high set point of norep (norepinephrine) are people whose brain 'engines' are set at a high idle. They are almost always revved up and ready to think." They also tend to speak quickly and at length and may be perceived as "high-strung" individuals. They may have difficulty "turning their brain off," so sleeping soundly could be a challenge. People in this category are logical "head types."

When engaging with prospects, if they appear to be intelligent thinkers and like numbers and technical or scientific data, enjoy learning how things work, are visionary or observational, talk nonstop, or are somewhat high strung, they are likely logical head types. While Aristotle advises us to balance our persuasion communications between logical, emotional, and instinctual arguments, we're best to adjust our styles based on types. In other words, add a bit more logical salt to your dialogue for this personality type. Also, this type gravitates toward more hands-on work, so they are most likely an evaluator persona.

Those with low levels of norep are referred to as the three instinctual "gut" personality types. They are more solid and steady, traditional and conventional, dependable and punctual, organized and confident, and "calm." Their thinking engines are not constantly engaged, so they rarely have a problem falling asleep. This type can be more peaceful, disciplined, commanding and controlling, easygoing, perfection oriented, and strong willed. They prefer bullet points, brief overviews, straight shooting, summarization, and more visual or auditory communications. Some numerical detail is fine, but not too much. They are motivated more by risk or harm avoidance and will often make fast gut decisions. They tend to gravitate toward leadership roles, so they are often decision-maker personas.

Schulze and Thomas determined that people with medium levels of norepinephrine fall into the emotional and feeling "heart" triad. They are "intermittent thinkers" and may cycle in and out of daydreaming. These types may also be more creative, moody, caring, goal oriented, helpful, driven, or empathetic. These types also prefer visual and auditory communications rather than lots of graphs, charts, or numbers. As they are "in the middle," they can play almost any role, but are more often influencer or decision-maker personas.

For marketers, while it's not an exact science, orienting messaging styles based on persona roles can be a good start. If prospects are more likely decision-makers, then use a more instinctual minimalist approach with bullets, summaries, and visual content. If evaluators, use a more logical detailed approach with more numbers, graphs, and lots of copy. If influencers, use a more middle ground emotional approach with a balance between the other two.

For sales pros, when initially engaging with a prospect, you can use similar approaches based on roles. The way prospects communicate can help you discern which triad approach to use. For example, if the prospect looks and acts more like an intelligent Einstein while talking at length and taking an interest in how things work, he or she is probably a logical type. If they're a bit impatient, stern, diplomatic, or not interested in the details but rather want you to "get to the point," they are likely more instinctual. If they smile a lot and want to open the conversation with lots of friendly "how's it going" talk about their dog and family, they're likely the more emotional type. These are general rules of thumb and not foolproof, but they will help you narrow in on *who* you're engaging so you can better tailor your conversation.

Once we know someone's triad profile, we can use a science-based storytelling approach to engage and persuade with far more success. Just as there are four parts to the three-act play, there are four steps to this process, subdivided by the three personas for decision-maker, evaluator, and influencer. Now let's have some fun by narrowing this down even more.

Schulze and Thomas went even deeper into the rabbit hole to show how individuals with high serotonin set points fall into another triad group called "positive outlook." Other researchers describe these individuals as playful, adventurous, and having positive orientations. They are more optimistic and tend to see the glass as half full instead of half empty. They often have warm, smiling personalities and appear to be "nice." They usually avoid confrontations or conflicts, are not into movies with lots of violence, and usually compromise rather than react or throw punches. They are usually helpful, peaceful, or adventurous. By the way, for companies running on EOS, Visionaries are often the more adventurous type. They can be excellent risk-taking entrepreneurs.

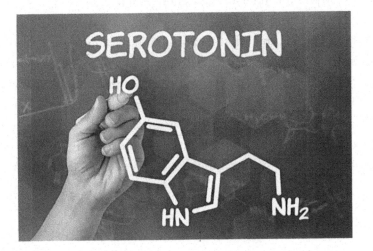

Those with low serotonin are just the opposite. They're fine with conflict, will defend themselves if attacked, and are more reactive. In other words, they have short fuses. They don't smile quite as much, are not quite as friendly, and may appear more aloof. They often tend to see the glass as half empty. They are usually strong and controlling, moody and creative, or loyal and security oriented. For companies running on EOS, this type can often gravitate toward the Integrator role.

Those with medium serotonin levels are, expectedly, in the middle. They are a mix of both the above and can lean either way with conflicts, violence, and warm and fuzzy things. They're a bit more practical, observant, and balanced. They tend to see a half-filled glass as being twice as tall as it needs to be. They are not as effusive as the high serotonin types, but also not as aloof as the low serotonin types. They are friendly, but not overly so. They are usually achievers and goal oriented, intellectual and observant, or judging and perfectionist types. They may do just fine as either an EOS Visionary or Integrator depending upon their interests.

It can be a bit harder for marketers to discern the difference between these three serotonin types based on personas, but like everything else, there's an app for that. It's a browser extension from RemotelyMe and uses AI and brain science to analyze a LinkedIn profile to determine personality profiles and communication preferences.

For sales or recruiting pros, this app allows you to quickly determine a prospect's profile and offers handy Communications Trust Playbooks with instructions, examples, and templates to adjust your communications style to connect, resonate, and persuade prospects. Also included is the ability to use data extracted from LinkedIn, such as experience, skills, and interests, combined with neuroscience-based profiling data, such as keywords to use, tone, style, etc., to prompt ChatGPT to create personalized emails, messages, phone scripts, and job descriptions.

CONCLUSIONS

- Our personalities are DNA hardwired, and did I mention that we're all insane?
- Everyone is either more emotional, instinctual, or logical...and also insane.
- Decision-makers are minimalistic because they have really small brains.

CHAPTER 16

4STORY

Selling is all about teaching.
And teaching is all about stories.

Why? Because Simon says so. Simon Sinek's *Start with Why* TED Talks have been viewed almost sixty million times. His concepts, when introduced many years ago, were revolutionary and are often reflected in sales, business, and marketing circles around the world. Sinek cites a few examples, such as Apple computer, wherein executives discovered the secret of reversing the typical messaging and strategy flow.

Many firms have adopted Sinek's approach, but many have not. Unlike Apple, the ones who have not start with What: we build great widgets. They progress to How: our widgets are great because we use the finest materials and cutting-edge technologies. Usually, they never get to Why. Apple, of course, goes the other direction. Why are we here and why should you buy our cool stuff? Because we want to revolutionize the way you work, play, and live. How? With the coolest technology on the planet that's super easy to use. With What? iPhones and Macs, of course.

Sounds simple, and in theory it is. However, as an executive consultant for dozens of leading firms across decades, I've seen the Why approach fail more times than it should. Why? Because companies did not start with *Who*. They still envisioned their firm and their stuff as the heroes of the story. They did not clearly identify Who they were trying to impact with their Why.

Yes, most marketers create go-to-market plans that outline the serviceable available market (SAM), target segments (geo, size, vertical markets, etc.), and personas (CEO, VP, decision-makers, etc.). However, this is only scratching the surface. Some organizations, mostly on the business-to-consumer (B2C) side of the fence, go a step further. They may create pictures of typical customers called John and Jane and place them on a wall. They discuss John and Jane's typical life, work, family, and day. They envision what these two are like and what they may want from a product, solution, or company. This is a great start, but to truly understand who these people are, we need to dive deeper. We need to make them the heroes of their story and outline their Heroes Journey in detail. Once we do engage with John and Jane, as recommended by *The Challenger Sale*, we need to teach, tailor, and take control of the sale.

I noted earlier that perhaps the above sequence is out of sequence. To teach anyone anything, we need to understand Who they are. We need to first tailor our teaching. Most teachers understand this concept, and many use a proven methodology called 4MAT. My sister, P. L. Reed, is also an author and began her career as a teacher. She earned a master's in educational science and studied and used the 4MAT system for more than a decade. In all, my family has delivered five teachers to the world, and most have used this system to some degree.

The 4MAT framework outlines four "learner types." Feelers/Watchers seek meaning and need to be personally involved. They learn by listening and sharing ideas and are interested in people, cultures, and social interaction. They are, obviously, more emotional.

Thinkers/Watchers seek and examine facts. They need to know what experts think and believe and are more interested in concepts and ideas. They like to collect data and examine information. They are analytical and function by adapting to experts. Certainly, they are more logical.

Thinkers/Doers and Feelers/Doers seek usability, learn by hands-on experience, prefer real-life correlation, enjoy variety and taking risks, and often reach conclusions without employing logic. Definitely they are more instinctual.

The 4MAT system recommends using different teaching methods to engage with each type, starting with the Feelers/Watchers. 4MAT uses a clockwise approach, beginning with personal relevance to ask the question Why. Teachers are encouraged to transition sequentially across the quadrants, progressing next to more rational concepts that will examine logical information that appeals to the Thinkers/Watchers. The second quadrant asks the question What.

The third quadrant appeals to the Thinkers/Doers who prefer hands-on experience and asks the question How. The final quadrant is more useful and impactful, asking the question What If, and will appeal to the Feelers/Doers.

As we know, this is a bit out of sequence with Sinek's *Start with Why*, which of course starts with Why and then goes to How and What. Sinek's path aligns better with storytelling, but both are missing the crucial first step: *Who*.

In the diagram below, we can see how modern neuroscience, storytelling, and alignment to popular sales methodologies can help us create a more modern and effective framework to ensure we not only engage properly with all learner types but do so using a storytelling structure to ensure much higher retention. As we learned earlier, studies conducted by the London Business School and others show a 1400 percent higher retention rate when we do this correctly. By overlaying the frameworks from Sinek, 4MAT, and most sales methodologies, and adjusting them to fit the three-act play, we create a new approach called 4STORY.

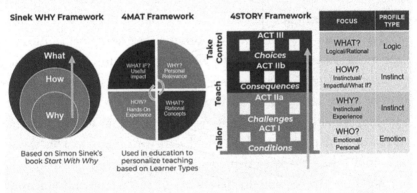

Start With Why and 4MAT alignment

© Copyright 2023. W. Craig Reed. All rights reserved

Virtually all writers select a genre: thriller, romance, sci-fi, memoir, historical, etc. They tailor their writing to this audience by completing months or years of research. Nonfiction writers create a proposal prior to writing a book that includes this research, outlines their target market (who), and then explains how they will appeal to and reach these readers. Fiction writers may not go this far, but they certainly consider the likes and dislikes of their target audience, and most ensure accuracy by interviewing experts and digging for facts. Diana Gabaldon in *Outlander*, for example, obviously researched Scottish, English, and French history before writing her bestsellers.

Many books begin with either a foreword or preface (nonfiction) or prologue (fiction) to pull in their audience. If a thriller, the prologue will usually begin with thrilling action. If historical nonfiction, the foreword or preface will introduce the book to readers who like this genre. In both cases, the first chapter, sentence, and words are carefully designed to grab and hold a target market's attention.

Long before a book is written or published, and then reflected in the first words on the page, writers seek to understand Who they are writing for. Likewise, before we can teach anyone anything, and therefore sell or market to these individuals, we need to know Who they are. We need to determine the learner types in our classroom. Are they an equal mix of all the types, or are most of them logical? If the latter, we may need to adjust our teaching style to focus a bit more on the What concepts.

Teachers use the 4MAT framework to create lesson plans. Business pros should likewise use the 4STORY framework to create messaging guides for collateral, emails, scripts, and so forth that include the equivalent of lesson plans. These plans should outline who we are teaching, why they should want to learn, how we are going to teach them, and what will be taught. Our plan should start with research. This should include the usual suspects: demographics, psychographics, etc., but go much further. To become the heroes of our story, John and Jane must be understood from every angle. While there are nine distinct profile types, as we now know, they are divided into three triads that are more emotional, logical, or instinctual. If we have the resources and time, we can create nine personas, but if not, three is a good start. You may also consider creating a matrix with three rows for the profile types (emotional, etc.) and three for the typical roles (influencer, evaluator, decision-maker). This equals nine fields, wherein we can outline details for each persona. Now we can start with the first story, or act, in our 4STORY building to complete the Buyer's Journey.

The first floor is Act I of the journey wherein we introduce our protagonist. We teach our readers Who the hero is by seeing them in an Ordinary World. Recall that every hero must have a quest, goal, or motivation for venturing into Act II. For each type, we should determine the optimal messaging, tone, graphics, and colors for our heroes to capture their attention and teach them something, while also motivating them to move beyond their comfort zones. The question now is, what do we teach them?

Do you recall what separates good books from great ones? It's called theme, and it's the important message writers want to convey to their audience. It's what they want to teach their readers. Great recruiters, marketers, and sales professionals also need to determine the theme. What is the most important message, or messages, we want to teach our candidates, prospects, or customers?

If we're Socrates, and we harken back to our example of deductive reasoning, our theme might be that *family comes first*. Our loved ones are more important than anything. We therefore want to teach people about life and death. Definitely a heavy topic, but if we're selling life insurance, it's not about rates or returns or even service. It's about dying.

Think about what impact your products or services have on your customers. Who are these people, why should they care, how can you change their lives, and what do you offer? Your theme should reflect this, but do so using only a few short sentences, like this:

Our theme is: There's no place like home.

Because there's no place like home, who will care about our insurance? People who say "family comes first," because they care about their home life. Why will they care? Because they want simple and uncomplicated lives so they can enjoy their families and then take care of them after they're gone. How can we help them attain this? With insurance policies that are uncomplicated and easy to understand. What do we offer? Life insurance.

As we can see, this approach maintains Sinek's initial ideas but simplifies and expands these. Now, we can create our 4STORY lesson plan to teach our optimal buyers. The goal of our lesson plan is to impart our theme while also imparting knowledge about our products and services and Why they can help our hero attain the theme. As such, our lesson plan should tell a great story.

In Act I, we tell the story about Jane in her Ordinary World. We learn Who she is and that she loves her home life, but something is missing. It's a bit gray and dull. Perhaps Jane is uncomfortable but she is not sure why. She meets a mentor, an older and wise gentleman who thrusts her into Act II with his own story about believing he'd live forever. See where we're headed? We begin with Who and move up from there. Along the way, our lesson plan teaches our audience what they need to know so that when they step into Act III, they understand why there's no place like home.

We'll wrap this chapter with an example of a story that can be used for sales enablement to teach a sales team and motivate them to engage with and close prospects.

Let's say we are a pharmaceutical firm and want to help our sales team embrace the passion and purpose that drives our company to succeed. We might use a story about a mother who was in a happy Ordinary World until her son, Johnny, was diagnosed with a serious disease. The disease has just become the antagonist. Mom got a call to action because of something the antagonist did, but she is so distraught she can't take that first step to explore treatment options. Finally, a nurse (mentor and friend) convinces her to embark on her Hero's Journey to find a cure for little Johnny.

The MacGuffin and magic elixir in our example story is, of course, the cure for Johnny. In Act II, the antagonist disease is progressing rapidly, and little Johnny is losing the battle. Cortisol and norepinephrine are increased in the brains of our audience. Mom is frantically exploring options but is thwarted at every turn by other bad guys. These might be snake oil companies who promise cures but then steal the money and disappear. Pacing is critical in this act. As we know, we should use more active verbs, shorter sentences, and paragraphs, and speed up the action. By the end of Act II, our heroine is finally pointed in the right direction by her mentor friend. The nurse did some research and found information about a miracle cure, and was "taught" about this cure by a sales rep from our pharmaceutical company. Spurred by her nurse friend,

Mom decides to look into our firm and the capability of our new drug designed to arrest this disease.

Our heroine mom learns more about the cure and wants to trust us, but she became so jaded and confused in Act II that she's not sure which choice to make. In the meantime, the doctors report that Johnny has precious little time left. In fact, they've discovered that there's now less time than previously thought. If they do not find a cure soon, Johnny will perish.

Mom is forced to dig deep and find an inner strength that she didn't know she had. She must now give it her all and do whatever it takes to save her son. She takes a leap of faith and decides to trust our firm to provide a treatment. At this late stage, there's no guarantees, but we are her best logical hope. In a thrilling climatic scene at the end of Act II, little Johnny almost doesn't make it but is saved in the last second by competent doctors and the medication provided by our company.

In Act III, we seek to offer calm assurance by raising serotonin and GABA levels in the brains of our audience. As we previously discovered, when we read a great mystery novel, we are amazed at how the protagonist logically brings together all the clues and facts and deductively catches the killer. In our story, Mom returns to her Ordinary World, with Johnny by her side, and is compelled to bring the "magical elixir," our medication, to all who reside there. She becomes an evangelist and spokesperson for the company and in time, thousands of lives are saved. How did this happen? Because one sales rep truly believed that our company's products can and will save lives. The rep became motivated to inform as many doctors and nurses as possible, and one of those nurses told our protagonist. Thus, little Johnny is alive, happy, and healthy.

If we can properly teach our sales teams to teach their prospects by using the 4STORY framework, we will not only fulfill our organization's mission, passion, and purpose, but we will also fill our bank accounts.

For more information on this framework and assistance in implementing this correctly, you can email admin@remotelyme.com or visit RemotelyMe.com/consulting.

CONCLUSIONS

- Simon Sinek didn't say so, but you should start with WHO and not with WHY.
- We pay attention to great stories; we fall asleep when boring politicians speak.
- The 4STORY framework is the best way to structure a great story that's not boring.

CHAPTER 17
CHANGE MANAGEMENT

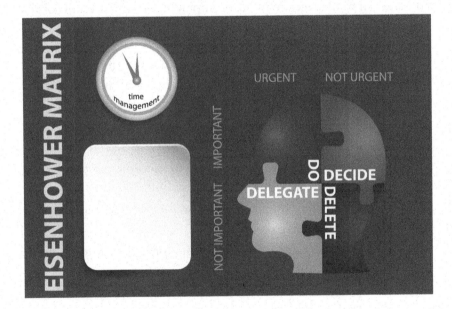

*"People are very open-minded about new things,
as long as they're exactly like the old ones."*
—Charles F. Kettering

B ecoming successful in business requires more than just implementing a few fancy new tricks. While the tricks in this book are
wicked cool and groundbreaking, they alone will not propel you

to stardom. We are not islands, and many others on our team will need to at least cooperate and accept the changes we suggest. This will not be easy, as most people resist change. To help others on your team embrace rather than roadblock change, you'll need to sell them on the benefits. This will require raising their oxytocin so they trust you and then focusing on what's important to implement the changes.

As previously noted, Dr. Paul Zak and others have shown that effectively raising oxytocin levels can increase trust and therefore cooperation. Zak conducted experiments showing the connection between raising oxytocin levels and increasing trust in work environments. He offered eight management behaviors that foster trust that are measurable and can be managed to improve employee performance and collaboration. I have paraphrased them below:

1. Recognize excellence—publicly reward top performers
2. Induce "challenge stress"—create moderate job stress via attainable goals
3. Ensure work autonomy—trust workers to complete projects in their own way
4. Enable job freedom—allow people to select the most rewarding projects
5. Share company information—a well-informed employee is a happier employee
6. Build relationships—less task orientation and more relationship orientation
7. Encourage wellness—facilitate personal growth along with professional growth
8. Show vulnerability—leaders should ask for help to encourage cooperation

You can use these approaches to foster trust, and then use a simple matrix to focus on the important change management tasks. *The 7 Habits of Highly Effective People* by Stephen R. Covey popularized a matrix grid with four quadrants called the time management grids. This matrix was created by President Dwight D. Eisenhower (Clear, 2014), who once said, "What is important is seldom urgent and what is urgent is seldom important."

Eisenhower placed tasks or projects that were urgent and important in the upper left quadrant of the matrix for immediate action. Items that were not urgent or important went into the upper right quadrant for further decision. Not important but urgent items went in the lower left for delegation, and not urgent and not important items went in the lower right for deletion.

This grid provides a simplified means to keep leadership priorities straight. However, Eisenhower created this grid decades before modern neuroscientists had a more mature understanding of how the human brain works. In today's dynamic and hectic world, leaders may need a better way to simplify projects and tasks and prioritize time.

Using a more neuroscientific approach to leadership decision-making, leaders might consider using three boxes to represent priority one, two, and three goals. Goal 1 is the most important goal required to accomplish a leader's purpose, vision, or mission identified for the organization, department, or team. This is similar to Eisenhower's urgent and important grid. Goal 2 is the second most important goal to reach this objective, which is similar to the not urgent and important grid. Goal 3 is similar to the urgent and not important grid. There is no box for not urgent and not important, as it is not needed.

Sales, marketing, recruiting, and other business leaders can then decide what percentage of their team's time will be devoted to each goal. Those with Lean and Six Sigma expertise often discuss the 80/20 Pareto principle, wherein 80 percent of the effects come from 20 percent of the causes. Translated for time management purposes, 80 percent of a team's time should be spent on 20 percent of the projects or tasks—those that will gain 80 percent of the objectives.

A leader might assign 60 to 65 percent of a team's time to goal 1, around 20 percent for goal 2, and 15 to 20 percent for goal 3. Note that goals 1 and 2 add up to about 80 percent, which aligns with the Pareto principle.

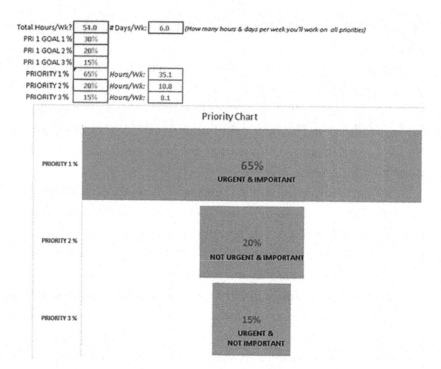

Psychologists and neuroscientists are beginning to understand what happens in the human mind (mental activity) and the brain (the physical region associated with the activity) when someone is required to make a decision (Schwartz and Thomson, 2016). Making decisions and forming habits is influenced by neuroplasticity principles discovered by Canadian scientist Donald Hebb in the 1950s. He created Hebb's law to summarize his findings: "Neurons that fire together wire together." Regions of the brain that are frequently activated in tandem will become physically associated with each another over time. The more often a mental activity pattern occurs, the more engrained the associated neural pathway becomes within the brain. Similar to a path that becomes worn through a forest by continued use, it becomes easier for the brain to traverse well-used neural pathways. This implies that the more one makes similar decisions, the more the brain's neural pathways will become accustomed to these types of decisions, making the decision-making task more automated over time.

Aristotle's Persuasion Model, as discussed earlier, suggests that humans need to engage all three parts of someone's brain to persuade them. Making a decision also requires persuasion. Leaders may need to persuade themselves that they are making the right and best decisions and then persuade their teams to execute on those decisions. The triune brain neuroscientific research we previously reviewed, as well as Aristotle's Persuasion Model, intimates that persuasion requires engaging all three areas of the human brain—logical, emotional, and instinctual.

To accomplish this with teams, leaders might draw three vertical lines on a whiteboard, a PowerPoint slide, or other visual aid to create three columns. They can label the first column "emotional," the second "instinctual," and the third "logical." In the emotional column, they should create purpose and passion statements that are emotional in nature, such as, "Our overarching purpose is to bring joy to millions of people by allowing them to connect and communicate easier by using our solutions."

They can then do the same in the instinctual column. They might write, "Our passion is to help our customers avoid risks and harm via solutions that offer greater security." Finally, they can list logical statements, such as, "Our goal is to provide affordable ways to connect by offering solutions that are 50 percent more efficient than others."

When making major decisions, leaders can place the document in a prominent location. They can then encourage brainstorming sessions with their team and list all decision ideas or points on a whiteboard. Once there are several decision points on the board, the team can examine each one against the backdrop of the firm's passion, purpose, and vision. They can then narrow the decision choices down to three finalists to simplify the process.

Now, leaders can draw two intersecting lines on the board, one vertical and one horizontal, to create four equal quadrants. They can label the upper left quadrant "emotional," the upper right one "instinctual," the lower right one "logical," and the lower left one "summary."

The team can examine decision possibility number one and, in the upper left quadrant, list three emotional reasons why this decision is a good one (fulfills the firm's purpose) and three reasons why it's bad. They can do the same for the instinctual and logical quadrants. The object of the exercise is to engage all three parts of everyone's brain to make more balanced decisions. Once the team has listed three good and bad reasons in each quadrant, they can rank each with a number between one and five, with five as the most important. For example, if reason number one resonates strongly (i.e., it aligns well with the passion and purpose), then the team can rate it as a five. They can use negative numbers for the three reasons they should not make this decision.

Once all the reasons have been scored, the team can select the most important "should do it" and "should not do it" reasons from each quadrant and place them in the fourth bottom left quadrant. Then, they can add up the positive numbers for the three "should do it" reasons and compare it to the sum of the negative "should not do it" numbers. If the "should do it" number is higher, they may consider that course of action. If not, they can eliminate that option and reevaluate.

In the visual example below, the decision to buy a convertible automobile (or not) is used. Some of the "should do it" reasons include less stress, lower repair risk, and high maintenance costs for the current car. One can compare those against the "should not" reasons of more stress, greater financial risk, and higher payments. In this example, the "should" reasons won, so the decision-maker should buy the convertible.

Neuron Decision Matrix

Should I buy a convertible?

1. Less Stress - 5
2. More Motivated - 5
3. More Fun - 3

1. More Guilt - 4
2. Bigger Ego - 3
3. More Stress - 5

1. Less Risk (Handling) - 3
2. Great Deal - 3
3. Less Risk (Maint) - 4

1. More Risk (Speed) - 3
2. More Risk (Financial) - 3
3. More Risk (Even Better Deal) - 2

13 —
1. Less Stress - 5
2. Less Risk (Maint) - 4
3. High Maint Cost - 4

12 —
1. More Stress - 5
2. More Risk (Fin) - 3
3. High Payments - 4

1. High Maint Cost (Current Car) - 4
2. Affordable in Budget - 3
3. Professional Need - 2

1. High Payments - 4
2. Sacrifice other Items - 3
3. Higher Cost (New vs Used) - 4

While neuroscientific studies and research are still nascent, and information relevant to its adaptation for leadership frameworks is virtually nonexistent, there are studies, books, papers, and research reports that leaders can leverage to create usable leadership strategies, frameworks, and models. Employing strategies to increase oxytocin to raise workplace trust, and increase dopamine to improve well-being and job satisfaction, have been shown to have positive and profitable results.

Using neuroscientific information to create models to make more effective decisions and better prioritize goals and time focus are two additional strategies that leaders can employ to improve productivity, attain organizational goals, and increase profitability.

SITUATIONAL LEADERSHIP

Decades ago, leadership researchers started analyzing the effects of introverted and extroverted managers, which led to research on specific leadership behaviors (Hersey and Blanchard, 1969, pp. 26–34). Researchers created two categories for task-oriented or relationship-oriented leaders.

Task-oriented leaders are seen to be more introverted and focused on getting the job done, completing tasks, or achieving goals. These leaders exhibit modest concern for employee relationships and place more emphasis on achievements, organization, and structure. The upside is higher productivity, but perhaps at the cost of morale, which can eventually affect productivity.

Relationship-oriented leaders are viewed as more extroverted and focus on people, relationships, teams, motivation, and support. They encourage collaboration and frequent communication and emphasize employee well-being and happiness. They understand that reducing workplace conflicts and stress can lead to higher productivity. The upside is higher morale and job satisfaction, but sometimes at the expense of productivity and profitability.

Researchers from Ohio State University and the University of Michigan published a series of studies in the 1950s that sought to determine which leadership style is more effective (Chong, 2017). They discovered that either style can be successful depending upon the situation. This led to a management approach called situational leadership, mentioned earlier and proffered by the Ken Blanchard Companies (co-author of *The New One Minute Manager*). This approach recommends that leaders should use either style depending upon who they are leading and when. They suggest that some people respond better to a task-oriented rather than a relationship-oriented style, and vice versa. This can also change depending upon the circumstances or situation. For example, if the firm has a critical deadline, a task style may be better. This can be an effective method of ensuring the proper leadership style is employed in a given situation.

The Ken Blanchard Companies also believe in a servant leadership model, wherein leaders serve subordinates by removing professional barriers to success and placing the needs, aspirations, and interests of others above their own (Sendjaya and Sarros, 2002, p. 57).

Based on the latest neuroscientific research, it may be possible to enhance or extend these approaches by ensuring that a leadership style or approach also aligns with a person's situation based on their neuroscientific personality, demeanor, and psychological health, as well as their role and responsibilities within a team unit. Most importantly, neuroscience teaches us that subordinates will more often do what a leader does rather than what a leader says. The reason for this may be related to mirror neurons.

As we learned earlier, mirror neurons were discovered in the 1980s by neuroscientist Dr. Giacomo Rizzolatti and his team from the University of Parma in Italy (Winderman, 2015, p. 48). Neuroscientists like Dr. Rizzolatti believe that mirror neurons play an important role in the learning process, which is why storytelling can be powerful. For leaders, an understanding of mirror neurons suggests the grave responsibility of setting the right examples. It may be easy to say, "Do what I say and not what I do," but the human brain may be wired to do just the opposite. It can therefore be important to maintain proper and good daily habits. Using mirror neurons, a leader's team may observe exhibited discipline, dedication, and actions and then emulate their leader.

McKinsey & Company, one of the world's most respected management consulting firms, determined that around 50 percent of cultural change management efforts fail when leaders do not set good examples by adopting the recommended changes or new behaviors (Boaz and Fox, 2014). The research conducted on mirror neurons appears to support this conclusion.

Plutarch was an ancient Greek educator and historian. He stated that most people, whether introverted or extroverted, prefer not to live in a vacuum. Instead, he believed humans are naturally curious and social creatures that imitate others through close observation. Plutarch taught how to accomplish this task through his famous biographical sketches, which pictorially told positive stories about Greek and Roman heroes, including Alexander the Great, Caesar Augustus, Cicero, Pericles, and others. His goal was to offer children examples of heroism they could emulate. Sans any knowledge about mirror neurons, Plutarch taught us how those we lead mirror what we do, not what we say.

The bottom line, or the net net, or whatever cool business phrase you prefer is this: better situational and servant leadership underscores any firm's ability to sell, market, recruit, and make money.

CONCLUSIONS

- Neuroplasticity helps us remember to recycle plastic.
- We should use a decision matrix to make a decision, then buy a new car anyway.
- Task-oriented leaders are mean; relationship-oriented leaders are nice but get fired.

CHAPTER 18
LEADERSHIP

*"It's hard to lead a cavalry charge if you
think you look funny on a horse."*
—Casey Stengel

O ver the past few decades, as an executive consultant and coach for
dozens of the world's largest and most innovative companies, I've
watched my clients spend millions with Big Five consulting firms

to implement change management or leadership development initiatives. Many months later, these consulting firms delivered comprehensive and detailed Lean Six Sigma road maps to a glorious future based on the latest management trends. That was the easy part. The hard part was inspiring individuals on each functional team, especially within recruiting, sales, and marketing departments, to willingly grab the keys and drive toward the destination on the map.

As we learned in the last chapter, implementing the concepts, ideas, frameworks, and best practices outlined in this book, or any book, requires change management underscored by effective leadership. A change management or leadership development road map outlines *what* we should do to get somewhere, but rarely does it address *how* we'll get there. Moreover, it does not usually articulate *why* we should go there in the first place, or even more importantly, *who* will go there and *who* will lead the charge. The real *why* is not about the perceived problems we need to rectify, it's about defining purpose and passion for those *who* are tasked with driving the change, which far transcends a simple mission statement. The *how* is not really about the individual process steps we will take to get there, it's about *how* we'll convince our teams to go there enthusiastically based on *who* they are. The *what* is not about a comprehensive process to drive more efficiency, it's about the foundational leadership principles the organization and its leaders embrace.

With a sincere desire to make a difference in our organization, many of us have hired consultants or read great leadership books written by excellent authors. We started following the advice of these experts, and perhaps we made some progress. Then we started taking one step forward and two steps back. Why?

Because we have lives and brains. Our lives often get in the way of our brains and vice versa. We're juggling kids, soccer games, piano lessons, PTA meetings, volunteer organizations, social engagements, and the demands of our profession. We're hammering out emails to San Francisco or Tel Aviv at 2:00 a.m. We want to start adopting that new leadership habit, but our busy lives make it nearly impossible to retrain our brain. Vanquishing our dusty old habits to adopt shiny new ones seems like an impossible task. How do we solve this problem?

Most leadership books focus on the latest skills, practices, and habits. These are important, but they are primarily outward-reflective qualities. The best leaders understand that you can't judge a book by its cover. The true quality of a book is found on its pages, not on its jacket. It's not enough to act like a leader. When we strip away the surface-level veneer that we display to the world, we must also embody the inner qualities of a leader down to the core of our being. It's not about *what* we do, it's about *who* we are.

WHAT'S THE PROBLEM?

Worldwide, bad leadership is costing organizations over $1 trillion each year.

A Gallup poll conducted years ago, before the pandemic, revealed that about 50 percent of the adults surveyed left a job to get away from a manager. A similar Gallup study of more than one million US workers found that the number one reason people quit their jobs is poor leadership.

Gallup *State of the American Workplace* studies have shocked US firms by revealing that only one-third of workers are engaged in their jobs, leaving more than two-thirds who are completely or partially disengaged. The estimated cost to US firms is over $500 billion each year in lost productivity and revenue. Given that only 48 percent of Americans have a full-time job, and only one-third are engaged, that means only 16 percent of the US population is actively *engaged* in full-time work. Similar statistics hold true for European and Asian firms.

Gallup studies have concluded that 77 percent of employees do not trust employers and nearly 80 percent are disengaged—which includes a new term called Quiet Quitting. A Barna Group study found that two in five Americans rank their boss as "bad," and just one in five assigns only positive attributes.

Researchers from Eastern Kentucky University's Bachelor of Science in Occupational Safety program uncovered that workplace stress is costing US firms $300 billion each year for health care and lost work days. They created an infographic showing that 77 percent of workers exhibit physical symptoms caused by work stress, and 60 percent said they wanted a new career.

Gallup estimates that based on average turnover rates, it could cost the typical 100-person company between $660,000 to $2.6 million for replacement expenses. Other studies show that one "bad apple" can have a domino effect that causes disruption and attrition. Over time, the damage can add up to almost $250,000 (Jörgen Sundberg Recruiting). Speaking of attrition, even without bad apples, almost half of all new hires fail or quit within eighteen months. More recently, they may "quiet quit" and fall into the highly unengaged category noted by Gallup.

An infographic created by *Inc.* magazine is eye opening. The title reads, "The Real Productivity-Killer: Jerks." *Inc.* infers that bad bosses aren't just a pain, they're bad for business. Colorful graphics in this report disclose that 65 percent of employees would choose a better boss over a pay raise. Around one-third confessed to dialing back their productivity due to poor leadership. The *Inc.* study concludes that it's not what bosses do that makes them bad, it's what they *don't* do.

The number one thing they don't do is inspire their teams. The number two thing they don't do is improve productivity—because they accept mediocrity. The number three thing is providing a clear vision, and number four is not being a good team leader, which is often directly related to trust issues.

Many experts believe that bad leadership is often related to a bad culture. A survey conducted on 200,000 employees across five hundred firms indicated that 71 percent of those organizations have mediocre to poor cultures, also directly related to trust.

Bad team leaders are not limited to the United States. The Chartered Institute of Management (CMI) found that almost half of all workers in the UK left at least one job solely because of a bad boss. In Australia, around two-thirds of workers who responded to a CareerOne survey rated their leaders as either "horrible" or "average."

Obviously, firms with bad leaders need to change, but so do many organizations with mostly good leaders. They need to change because everything around them is changing. They need to change because the difference between good leadership and great leadership could equate to tens or even hundreds of millions in profit.

Leaders who recognize the need to change, and are courageous enough to do so, can learn a great deal about leadership from three excellent sources of wisdom.

WHAT CAN LEADERS LEARN FROM NEUROSCIENTISTS?

One of the fastest supercomputers in the world is China's Tianhe. This beast has 18,000 times more moxie than your Sony PlayStation and is 400,000 times faster than most iPhones, but it will never know sadness, kindness, or joy. It will never understand the meaning of hope, failure, or inspiration. And it will never feel happiness, fear, or love. It will never be able to lead or inspire teams, because human beings aren't computers. Trying to lead people without a thorough understanding of how their brains work is like trying to become a golf pro without learning how to properly swing a club. Some leaders are naturally gifted and may do well, but rarely does someone make it to the pros without studying the science of the swing.

The science behind the "leadership swing" is called neuroscience.

Some of the world's top neuroscientists, many of whom are associated with leading institutions like Harvard University, have made startling discoveries in the last decade about the human brain. Some of these insights can help leaders dramatically improve employee morale, productivity, trust, and retention. For example, we learned in this book that increasing oxytocin can enhance trust and customer brand loyalty. Dozens of blue chip firms have also discovered that employing neuromarketing principles can offer marketers the equivalent of a flashlight and a road map into the decision-making centers of a customer's brain, but it can also dramatically improve our ability to lead teams.

WHAT CAN LEADERS LEARN FROM THE ANCIENT GREEKS?

The Greeks knew more about love and each other than we do. The modern world uses only one word for love; the ancient Greeks used seven. For some readers, approaching leadership development from the perspective of "love" may seem a bit too touchy-feely. Shouldn't we focus on the net net and the bottom line and quarterly business reviews?

For those who see a disconnect between business and the science of love—including an understanding of why employees love their jobs and customers love your brand—I recommend a great business book titled *Conscious Capitalism*, co-written by John Mackey, the co-founder of Whole Foods Market. In this popular book, Mackey explains why firms that have a passion and purpose and aspire to make an impact rather than only money often financially outperform competitors by a factor of eleven to one on Wall Street.

The bottom line is that the Greeks have a lot to teach us about the net net.

WHAT CAN LEADERS LEARN FROM MILITARY COMMANDERS?

Before John F. Kennedy was president of the United States, he was a naval officer and the skipper of motor torpedo boat PT-109 serving in the Pacific during World War II. He commanded a crew of two officers and fourteen sailors. These brave men charged headlong toward enemy warships that carried orders of magnitude more firepower.

One fateful night, Kennedy's PT-109 was accidentally sliced in two by a Japanese destroyer. Kennedy led his team by example. He towed a badly burned enlisted man for four hours to reach a nearby island and encouraged his men to help each other through their difficult ordeal. They were stranded on the island for almost a week, surviving on only coconuts and Kennedy's strong leadership. Many say this near-death experience helped to create one of the most iconic and inspirational leaders of our time. Those who have served in small military units understand that team leadership does not start with a catastrophe. It starts with camaraderie, respect, and teamwork.

In modern society, experts now agree that the bottom-up and top-down leadership models of the past are no longer effective. In today's fast-paced, internationally diverse, and internet-driven society, we need an entirely new form of team leadership that empowers each person on the team to contribute as leaders in the most optimal way. The best team leadership examples can be found in tight military units such as special operations units, submarines, air squadrons, and PT boats.

INSPIRATION, NOT COERCION

The Greek philosopher Heraclitus once said, "No man ever steps in the same river twice, for it's not the same river, and he's not the same man." The speed of business today makes it impossible to stand still. The river of life will pass us by. To be successful leaders, we must continuously improve our knowledge and skills lest we become obsolete, worthless, and penniless.

That said, if your only motivation to become a better team leader is to make more money, you may want to consider some healthy introspection. Increased revenue and market share may well be the by-product of improved leadership, but it should not be our only goal. This book, and any other, does not offer a magical pair of slippers that can be clicked three times to find your way across a rainbow or to a pot of gold. It is not a get-rich-quick scheme or an instructional manual on how to bend the universe and everyone in it to your will. You will not consistently invoke positive change by manipulation, coercion, deceit, or force. People need to be inspired, not compelled.

Rather than focus outwardly on trying to change everyone else, great leaders seek to change themselves. They understand that we must first make the appropriate and wise changes to *our* life, to *our* reactions, to *our* expectations, to *our* attitudes, to *our* communication style, to *our* mind and heart, and to *our* leadership style. We will then see a magical change in *us*—and perhaps in *everyone* we lead.

MENTORING FOR MANAGERS

Lance De Jong served as vice president of North American sales for Oracle. He concurs that it's important for leaders to care for the members of their team, and a good way to do that is to generously offer your time and wisdom as a mentor. He recalls, earlier in his career, being mentored by a man named John who informed Lance that if he wanted to be mentored, he had to abide by three rules. One, Lance had to bring the questions to John. This forced Lance to do his homework and come prepared with questions for his mentor. Two, Lance had to honor and respect the time commitment. They would never cancel or reschedule unless a life-threatening situation forced them to do so. Three, Lance needed to be a river and not a reservoir. He had to agree to pass on what he'd learned from John to someone else.

"In my first lesson with John," Lance says, "he challenged me to do my homework and write down and memorize my primary six core values. What did I stand for? What defined me? I thought I knew, but John taught me how to dig deeper and really understand who I was."

John's mentorship helped Lance formulate his three pillars of leadership. Of most importance is trust, which forms the backbone of everything he does. Lance defines the second pillar with one word: serve. His philosophy is to flip an organizational chart upside down and determine how he can add value to his direct reports and their teams. In his opinion, if he is not finding ways to help his team, he is not doing his job effectively. The third pillar is caring.

"You must find a way to show your people that you genuinely care about them," says Lance. "It can't be phony. It must be authentic."

Lance believes that effective leaders should constantly ask themselves three important questions: One, are the people you are leading following you and how do you know? Two, is your team growing personally and professionally and how do you know? And three, are the people you are leading succeeding and how do you know?

"There's a big difference between a manager and a leader," says Lance. "If I were a CEO, I'd strive to nurture leaders, not managers."

Lance reported to a manager, we'll call him Fred, who had a military background. While Lance knows that the military can and has produced some great leaders, a few have emerged as more managers than leaders, and Fred fell into this category. He was an invasive micromanager who managed by spreadsheets and made Lance feel untrusted. When challenged, Fred got defensive, raised his voice, and demanded respect. Rather than argue with Fred, Lance instead tried to understand. He recognized that Fred did not feel safe, so Lance said, "I respect you and I'm glad you brought this up." He then endeavored to earn Fred's trust while not compromising his own principles or acting like a doormat. During this experience, Lance learned a valuable lesson about "leading up."

Lance admonishes aspiring leaders to do as he did while being mentored by John. First, understand *who* you are by knowing what you are deeply passionate about and *not* passionate about. How do you believe your talents will help you accel, and in what areas? Also, set clear and attainable goals that will help you stretch and gain confidence.

"I think it's important to turn aspiring leaders into leaders of leaders," says Lance. "Leading is all about relationships, not tasks. You must have someone's permission to lead them. Others will follow you if they believe you can help transform them into what they want to become."

Vision and inspiration are two key components that Lance feels are vital to help your team transform. You must impart a clear vision that incorporates a worthwhile overarching passion and purpose beyond only profits. Then, inspire others to reach for those stars. Team diversity is also important, along with open communication and healthy arguments.

"A team with 'five Lances' is not a good thing," says Lance. "I much prefer a diverse team where everyone has different strengths, personalities, and opinions. The sum of our parts makes us greater as a whole."

Lance believes that as a society we are starving for strong, effective, and inspirational leadership. We have the opportunity to lead in almost every aspect of our lives. Leadership is not something that is gifted to us, it is something we can choose to learn and to earn. We become leaders not by stepping on others as we climb the ladder to success but by the choices we make and how we treat others with generosity, caring, and respect.

PASSION AND PURPOSE

Lenny Alugas grew up in New Orleans, earned an engineering degree, and was later recruited by Hewlett-Packard as a presales engineer. Seventeen years later, Lenny was running a $160 million business unit with six hundred employees. While there, he became a big fan of HP's leadership development programs and philosophies.

"HP had a well-defined and excellent set of core values," says Lenny. "They believed in an open-door policy with their leaders and encouraged managers to walk around and observe their environment. They had a strong desire to create effective teams where people could thrive."

Lenny recalls that HP considers their number one passion to be customers and employees. Even today, on the HP "About Us" web page, the company leads with a quote from Dave Packard about the necessity of people working together toward common objectives.

HPE says their culture is what defines them as a company in terms of how they act, how they treat others, and how they conduct business. They also indicate that a commitment to employees and leadership skills are top corporate objectives. These philosophies are apparently working. HP is consistently listed by Forbes as one of the top ten technology firms in the world.

"When you received a pay raise at HP, they gave you a printout with all the information on it," says Lenny. "That wasn't good enough for my boss, Paul Hansen. He always handwrote a personal note on that paper to congratulate me and thank me for my hard work. That meant a lot to me. Twenty-five-years later, I still have copies of those notes."

Lenny enjoyed his time at HP, but after many years he decided to explore the world of a start-up. He joined Veritas in the early nineties and helped drive the company toward success and an acquisition twelve years later by Symantec. At one point, Lenny was managing a $4 billion maintenance facility with thousands of employees.

"Symantec also had some excellent leaders," says Lenny. "I enjoyed working for our CEO, Steve Bennett, who came from General Electric. He had an incredible leadership philosophy. I resonated with his beliefs that leaders should communicate the firm's mission, strategy, and goals clearly and ensure employees are inspired to attain them. Also, he felt it was important to develop personal character at every level."

Lenny also praised Bennett's philosophies that good leaders need to have the courage to make decisions and teach their team members how to do the same. Bennett indicated that it was vitally important to treat employees as if they were valuable investments. He encouraged his direct reports to keep at least 30 to 40 percent of their time free so they could invest time in their people.

"I learned several valuable lessons from the leaders I worked for at HP and Symantec," says Lenny. "Most importantly, I learned that it's vital to develop a strategy, mission, and vision that aligns with your passion and purpose, and communicate those clearly and effectively to your entire team. Then, inspire your team to work together to achieve the vision."

FLYING HIGH ON PASSION

Sangita Woerner grew up in a traditional Asian Indian household. Both of her parents were first generation and immigrated to America before she was born. Sangita's mother was a stay-at-home mom and her father worked for Ford Motor Company throughout his career. He advised her that the two most reliable career paths were engineering or accounting. She decided to pursue the latter.

After graduating from college with an accounting degree, Sangita eventually discovered marketing and worked her way up the ladder to a vice president of marketing position at Starbucks. She then became the vice president of marketing for Alaska Airlines, where she empowered, motivated, and guided her team toward success. Aspiring leaders at Alaska Airlines often speak of Sangita with admiration as they try to emulate her leadership style and approach.

Sangita advises her team, as well as up-and-coming leaders, to focus on what's important. Almost every leader can be challenged by dozens of problems, tasks, and distractions daily. Discerning which ones to focus on at any given time takes practice, patience, and an open mind.

"I think it's critical to listen to your team, colleagues, customers, and mentors. Their input can help you determine proper priorities and make informed decisions."

Sangita recalls being encouraged by a mentor to refrain from focusing only on results and spend more time turning her head from side to side. He advised her that she was not spending enough time building relationships and ensuring that she was in step with her team on the journey toward their goals.

"He said that I couldn't end up on the finish line alone," says Sangita. "I needed to run the race alongside my team and colleagues. By fostering closer relationships, I'd be rewarded with diverse perspectives and insights and perhaps more efficient paths to reach our goals. Every person can bring something unique and special to the table because we all have different backgrounds, expertise, and viewpoints.

"A leader can accomplish far more with the help and support of an empowered and impassioned team," says Sangita. "While it's important to remain focused on a grand vision, sometimes it's just as important to focus on what you and your team can accomplish on a smaller scale every day."

CUSTOMERS ARE HEROES

Janani Nagarajan is the senior director of product marketing for CrowdStrike, a leading cybersecurity company. Like me, she was short-listed as a top nine finalist by the Product Marketing Association (PMA) for the Messaging and Positioning Maestro of the Year award. Neither of us won, but given PMA's 30,000+ membership, being shortlisted was quite an honor. Also like me, Janani is a strong proponent of proper storytelling for sales and marketing messaging.

"Too often I see marketing and sales professionals create presentations for customers that begin with several slides about their company, accolades, and customer logos," says Janani. "I disagree with this approach, as it makes the company the hero of the story and not the customer. A good story starts by introducing the hero, which is the customer, and concludes with the hero making right choices to solve their problems. Information about our company and our awards belongs at the end of the story, not the beginning."

Janani obviously knows what's she talking about. Although she has a technical background, having earned a master's in electrical engineering from the University of Texas at Dallas, she has a long and successful career in marketing. She previously worked at Cisco and joined CrowdStrike when they only had a handful of products. With her help, the company earned a reputation as an industry leader and skyrocketed to dozens of leading products within a few years. By understanding who she is trying to persuade, and making them the hero of the story, she has helped herself and her company become heroes as well.

THE SCIENCE OF MARKETING

Speaking of the PMA, Harvey Lee is the vice president of product marketing for the organization, which is based in London, England. Harvey notes that product marketing as a discipline is a subset of marketing, which in his opinion was invented by Procter & Gamble in 1931. That year, P&G introduced a new concept called "brand management," which focused more on product differentiation and specialization rather than business functions. By distinguishing individual characteristics and values for each brand from all others, and by targeting different consumer personas, they avoided internal competition for mindshare and wallets.

"Back then, the brand manager did everything," says Harvey with a polished British accent. "Today, functions are fragmented across multiple areas, including demand generation, communications, branding, content, digital, analyst relations, product management, and product marketing."

According to Harvey, product marketing management (PMM) has only become a known entity within the last fifteen years. Having co-founded Aventi Group, one of the first product marketing consulting firms that became an *Inc.* 5000 company, I can attest that PMM as a discipline is still in its infancy.

"Over 90 percent of the PMMs with the PMA are with business-to-business (B2B) firms rather than business-to-consumer (B2C). They typically focus on segmentation, positioning, personas, and messaging. Unfortunately, given the lack of frameworks, training courses, and guidance specific to the PMM discipline, many PMMs struggle or fail."

Harvey concurs that B2C firms often have an edge, as they are far ahead of B2B firms when it comes to using neuroscience and storytelling. While many B2C companies often use neuromarketing, few marketers at B2B organizations understand the meaning of the term. For example, Microsoft and IBM use eye-tracking techniques to understand customer tendencies so they can improve product displays. Apple designs products based on tests that verify the release of specific neurotransmitters when customers handle and use an iPhone or Mac. Many other firms, including P&G, Porsche, HP, Volvo, and Budweiser, rely on neuromarketing to improve ads, products, and messaging. However, these are all for B2C products.

"Product marketing is young, and so are most product marketers," Harvey says. "Only half of all marketers have a marketing degree, over 65 percent of PMMs are junior with less than five years' experience, and 35 percent have less than three years. They are barely becoming experts at basic PMM functions, so they may not be ready to employ better storytelling or use neuroscience."

Harvey notes that most PMMs are "accidental." In fact, his own path to a VP PMM was never planned. He launched his career in the music business as a label manager for a record company, which led to a role in marketing for an artist management firm in London. He was fortunate to be selected for an opportunity at Microsoft as part of a small team that launched the first Xbox gaming console. He later did a stint at Epson before assuming a VP role at the PMA.

"Storytelling and alignment with sales frameworks can be critical to the success of any company's messaging, sales enablement, and asset creation," says Harvey. "Unfortunately, most PMMs and executives have very little knowledge, training, or experience in this area. This is especially true for technology firms that insist on creating presentation slides covered with detailed technical diagrams and more text than a novel."

Harvey recommends that all marketers, and especially product marketers and sales enablement professionals, get certified in three areas: product marketing or account-based marketing (ABM), storytelling, and sales enablement or sales. The PMA offers several excellent PMM courses and certifications, as does RemotelyMe, which offers courses and apps for storytelling and sales, including their renowned FROG Selling Course based on the principles in this book.

FACTS TELL, STORIES SELL

Indy Bains is the vice president of industry and solution marketing at Workday, a leader in the human resources software market with over sixty million users across almost 10,000 companies worldwide. Prior to Workday, Indy spent over two decades at Oracle. Like Harvey Lee at the PMA, Indy accidentally stepped into marketing.

"I originally wanted to be a CPA," says Indy. "I started my career in finance, but that eventually led me toward presenting and messaging, and then into marketing."

Indy sees storytelling as more an art than a science that requires understanding who we are communicating with. He believes marketers should spend more time with sales professionals and customers to understand who is buying and why they care about specific solutions...or not. "Marketers need to be aligned with sales teams," says Indy. "PMMs should invest in relationships and seek input from stakeholders."

As a marketer for a large HR technology firm, Indy also sees the need to improve the employee hiring and retention process at many companies. "Retention, employee engagement, and talent acquisition have become large issues at many organizations," says Indy. "Hybrid work has changed the game, and we need better solutions to find, assess, and retain the best workers."

Workday, of course, offers industry-leading solutions to help with this, including a Human Resources Information System (HRIS) that many HR professionals swear by. It handles all aspects of employee HR planning, employee experience, employee engagement, and people analytics. Workday's Enterprise Management Cloud also includes solutions for finance, HR, planning, and spend management.

RemotelyMe's platform integrates with and augments Workday by using groundbreaking visual neuroscience storytelling assessments based on the concepts I've written about in my books. As we learned earlier, we have three brains that are more logical, emotional, and instinctual. Also, our emotional and instinctual brains are responsible for over 90 percent of our decision-making and prefer video, graphics, and sounds. This is a problem for nearly all personality and employee assessments, as they use text and word-based tests. You're asking someone to make decisions about who they are by only speaking to 10 percent of their decision-making brain. That's why virtually all of these tests have low accuracy and a 30 percent completion rate on average. RemotelyMe's approach appeals to 100 percent of the decision-making brain and therefore has a 97 percent completion rate and proven 93 percent validity.

CONCLUSIONS

- Leaders lead, followers follow, everyone else whines and complains.
- The best leaders care about others; the worst leaders only care about themselves.

- Leaders lead through persuasion, which requires wearing fancy bedsheets.

"There's no such thing as a bad case study. However, they are far better when we tell a good story. The first paragraph should introduce the hero and then place the reader in their shoes. Science can improve our stories, especially related to images our eyes are drawn to."

—Erik Mansur, Head of Product
Marketing, Ziflow (formerly Crayon)

"We need to invest far more in learning how to tell proper stories, and in teaching our sales teams how to do this."

—Kirstin Jepson, Senior Director Product
Marketing, Telus International

CHAPTER 19
TRACTION

*"You can't have a million-dollar business dream
with a minimum-wage work ethic."*
—Stephen C. Hogan

n the foreword to this book, EOS Visionaries Mike Paton and
Mark O'Donnell described Gino Wickman's vision to create the
Entrepreneurial Operating System, now in use by over 150,000

companies around the globe. During EOS Worldwide's formative years, *Traction* author Gino Wickman served as the company's Visionary and, functionally, as CEO. To help firms "get it right" and properly embrace the EOS model, Wickman created a team of channel partners called EOS Implementers. These are independent contractors, most who were successful entrepreneurs and used EOS to thrive and grow. Along the way, they discovered their own passion and purpose—to help others use EOS to ensure everyone in their small business is "singing off the same song sheet." Perhaps more importantly, that everyone is singing in tune.

There are now around 600 EOS Implementers who help 20,000 clients live their dreams. Following the instructions outlined in Wickman's books, these Implementers show clients how to define core values and core focus. For example, EOS Worldwide's five core values are Be Humbly Confident, Grow or Die, Help First, Do the Right Thing, and Do What You Say.

The EOS model consists of the Six Key Components that, according to the book *Traction*, "must be managed and strengthened to create a healthy, well-run business." These are:

> **Vision**—clearly defining who and what your organization is, where it's going, and how it's going to get there.

> **People**—getting the right people in the right seats.

> **Data**—using key metrics to give the team a clear pulse on where things are, and when they are off track.

> **Issues**—strengthening your organization's ability to identify issues, address them, and make them go away forever.

> **Process**—systemizing your business by identifying and documenting the core processes that define the way to run your firm.

Traction—the ability for business leaders to execute well and bring focus, accountability, and discipline to their organization.

THE EOS MODEL™

Implementers also guide clients toward finding the right customers for the right solutions by creating marketing strategies, as well as three "uniques," defined as what your firm uniquely offers to customers. From there, teams can use the People Analyzer to ensure the right people are in the right seats. They are encouraged to score current and prospective employees based on whether they Get It (Intuition), Want It (Inclination), and have the Capacity to Do It (Intellect). Teams use a simple plus, minus, or plus/minus score for each of these GWC categories. If someone has a minus for any area, they may not be the right fit for that seat. If they don't resonate with and embrace the firm's core values, they will likely not be happy, fulfilled, and motivated enough to shovel coal into the company's engine each day.

Eventually, and as planned, Wickman handed EOS Worldwide's steering wheel to Mike Paton, who transitioned into the Visionary role after eight years as an EOS Implementer. Having grown up in an entrepreneurial household, Paton cut his teeth in banking before embarking on his own entrepreneurial journey—four stints running (or helping run) small, growing businesses. As with most entrepreneurial leaders, Paton and his companies experienced some successes and plenty of failures, the last of which led to his discovery of EOS.

"Most of my struggles—and those of my fellow leaders at these companies—were caused by misalignment," says Paton. "We hadn't spent enough time clarifying our company's vision, the culture we wanted to build together, or what we expected from one another."

When a neighbor shared his recently published copy of *Traction* with Paton, he quickly saw how EOS could help even successful businesses and leaders get better. Within a few months, he'd become a zealot, building a successful practice helping entrepreneurs in the Twin Cities run better businesses and live better lives. In 2012, he and Wickman co-authored the second book in the Traction Library, *Get a Grip* (a business fable), and when Wickman stepped down, Paton stepped up. In his five years as its Visionary, EOS Worldwide's community of professional implementers grew from sixty to more than three hundred around the globe.

"I enjoyed the role," Paton explains, "but in the end I recognized that the company needed more than I was able to give. Plus, I realized that my true calling is working in the trenches with leaders and leadership teams."

He now spends all his time writing (he and co-author Lisa Gonzalez recently published *Process!*, the seventh book in the Traction Library), conducting talks and workshops and helping his clients run their businesses on EOS.

Very early in that journey, Paton helps teams clearly articulate and align around their company's vision. "It starts with discovering and defining the organization's core values," he explains. "When a team is crystal clear on the kind of people around whom they want to build a strong and unique culture, it's far easier to attract and retain those folks, and to repel everyone else. I know firsthand how hard it is to do that, so this work is extremely rewarding."

Each core value is crafted to be short, memorable, and clearly defined. "For example," he says, "EOS Worldwide's core value 'Grow or Die' packs a lot of punch into three simple words, and it leaves no room for interpretation."

Once defined, core values are brought to life by using them every day to hire, fire, review, reward, and recognize people. "If you don't live and breathe your core values," Paton explains, "they'll die on the vine. Putting them behind the reception desk or on the website is fine, but it's not going to help you build a great culture. You've got to walk the talk. Follow them yourself, of course. Use them so frequently that you're almost sick of them, and then do it some more. The people who don't fit your culture will self-select out; the employees who do fit will love working there so much they attract other people just like them."

While serving as a submariner and US Navy diver, occasionally on joint missions with SEAL Team One, and having interviewed hundreds of military veterans, I've learned well the meaning of "foxhole buddy." This term refers to the battlefield view that while you may be fighting for ideologies and nations, you're more often willing to face bullets or bombs for the person on your right or left. Even if you don't know them well, or perhaps even like them, you're willing to risk your life for them because you know they're willing to do the same. You share common bonds, goals, and risks. You share the same core values.

The same principle can hold true for many organizations, especially when small. The best teams foster bonds of trust and act like well-oiled machines, with the wheels turning in sync.

"The best EOS companies follow a rigorous process for hiring," says Paton. "They initially use EOS Tools like the Accountability Chart, the People Analyzer, and GWC to evaluate current employees to understand who is a 'right person' (which means they fit the company's culture) and is 'in the right seat' (meaning they're great at their job). Companies running on EOS also use these tools to screen and select prospective candidates—often employing assessment tools to gather additional data."

According to Paton, Kolbe assessments are popular when combined with well-defined processes for interviewing and determining core values and culture fit. While the Kolbe methodology was cutting-edge two decades ago when invented, the more recent changes noted in the introduction to this book have altered our current workforce and workplace dynamics. Paton also mentions a more recent solution from author Patrick Lencioni called the Six Working Geniuses. This solution, like most others, relies on behavioral observations and uses forty-two text-based questions.

"Data is one of the Six Key Components in the EOS model," says Paton. "Gathering, tracking, and properly using the right metrics can help ensure better decision-making for people selection, as well as for other important areas of your business."

As his clients mature, Paton sees many begin to rely on human resources information systems (HRIS) or applicant tracking systems (ATS), such as Workday or BambooHR. Whether ready for those tools or not, he believes that leaders and companies who compile and use data will make better, faster decisions around people and therefore be likely to outpace the competition.

Another question leadership teams answer when clearly defining the company's vision is, "What is our marketing strategy?" This simple, high-level question is answered in four parts. The company's target market is a definition of an ideal prospect—the demographic, geographic, and psychographic profile of the people or companies most likely to become great customers. The next three parts of the marketing strategy—3 Uniques, Proven Process, and Guarantee—comprise the firm's ideal marketing message.

"All we're doing here is getting the whole team involved in the process of determining where and how to invest our precious few marketing and sales dollars to generate the biggest return," Paton explains. "Some of our clients ultimately go a lot deeper—building more detailed prospect personas or customer journeys, for example. But for any marketing strategy to truly work, you've got to agree on these high-level elements first."

As we learned earlier, Aristotle also discovered that persuading someone requires going beyond only logic by also speaking to someone's emotional and instinctual brain. We now know that the latter two are critical, as most of our decisions are not logical. Crafting the right marketing strategy helps entrepreneurial companies tell a more compelling story to the right prospective buyers, which vastly improves a company's return on its sales and marketing investment.

In their book *Process!*, Paton and Gonzalez also make a strong case for consistent execution of a carefully crafted marketing and sales process. Paton sees some clients tap into a proven sales framework such as Miller Heiman, Sandler, or *The Challenger Sale*, but most companies running on EOS are able to quickly improve results by developing and getting their own marketing and sales processes "FBA," or "followed by all."

"We wrote the book to help entrepreneurs embrace the key component most of us resist," he says. "Too many entrepreneurs believe you have to choose between an entrepreneurial company and one that is process-driven. We know the opposite is true—that the most entrepreneurial companies embrace process—which frees their leaders up to create, disrupt, or innovate. Without process, those same leaders would be sucked into the day-to-day—cleaning up messes, putting out fires, and gradually losing their passion for the business."

That is Paton's ultimate message for the amazing people who own or lead small, growing companies. "Never lose your passion for the business," he implores. "Stay connected to the reason you started the business in the first place, and be clear and specific about what you want from it in the future. Share that vision with everyone you know, especially those in the business who are essential to helping you achieve it. And when your passion starts to wane or you're not having fun—ask for help."

Systems like EOS can help, but Paton does not believe every business needs to run on EOS. Instead, he recommends finding and adopting a system or approach to running your business that works for you. So while adopting EOS isn't the only answer, it's been proven as one of the best. There must be a reason why over 150,000 companies worldwide are using the EOS Tools.

TODAY'S VISIONARY

Mark O'Donnell is the current Visionary for EOS Worldwide. He essentially operates as the firm's CEO, but EOS companies view titles somewhat differently. As noted earlier, Visionaries function as the title intimates, helping their firms attain success by seeing and driving toward the overall long-term vision. Post-college, Mark launched his career in pharmaceuticals working for Johnson & Johnson and then GlaxoSmithKline. During the recession in 2007, Mark and his brother elected to become entrepreneurial risk-takers by starting their own consulting business for biotechnology and pharmaceutical firms. Demand was high, and the company grew from only two co-founders to twenty-three employees within six months.

Across the next few years, they skyrocketed to $30 million in annual revenue and merged with another company, thereby adding two more partners. While expanding globally across nine distinct businesses, Mark completed his master of business administration (MBA) and decided it was time to better integrate the various entities into one cohesive unit. He and his partners worked well together but were often not on the same page when it came to key decisions and business direction.

"My MBA school provided an excellent education," says Mark, "but it did not offer the answers we needed to run nine harmonious businesses with multiple partners. I read several books and tried a few approaches, but none of them worked. Finally, I found Gino Wickman's book *Traction*, read the first chapter, and was hooked. I started dabbling with a few of the concepts in the book but was only getting my feet wet when an interesting coincidence propelled me forward."

Mark and his partners had been selected as representative business owners for a small business advisory council sponsored by President Barack Obama's administration. While at the White House in Washington, DC, Mark met with a small business advisor name Jonathan Smith. Mark later learned that Smith was as an EOS Implementer.

"I raised an eyebrow, as I was in the middle of reading about EOS companies in the book *Traction*," says Mark. "However, I did not yet know that EOS Worldwide had Implementers, or coaches, who could consult with companies to help them implement EOS processes."

Mark and his partners hired Smith to help them implement EOS across their businesses. The results were immediate and transformational.

"I fell in love with the EOS concepts imparted by Smith and started seeing true empowerment and enablement with leaders in our various companies."

Mark decided to attend EOS "boot camp," where he met other business owners while diving deeper into the EOS concepts. When an opportunity to help another firm implement EOS landed on Mark's doorstep, that led to an interest in becoming an EOS Implementer.

"While teaching a small business how to use the EOS system," Mark says, "I found my true passion and purpose in life. I loved every minute of it."

Mark become an EOS Implementer in 2015 and sold his other companies a few years later. He helped over one hundred clients and then started coaching other Implementers before stepping into the role of Visionary for EOS Worldwide in 2020.

"EOS offers business leaders hope, clarity, and freedom," says Mark. "When they begin to see the light at the end of the tunnel, they have hope. As the momentum carries them forward, they gain clarity of vision, people, and uniqueness. Finally, as they leverage data, structure, and processes, they find freedom and, in many cases, relief from stress and fear."

Mark notes that not all businesses fully embrace the EOS way, but when they do—especially if they work with an Implementer—miracles can happen. Business owners can become better leaders, and when the proverbial weights are lifted from shoulders, they can also become better spouses, parents, and friends. Their businesses operate more smoothly, drive more revenue, and attract the best people. Obviously, when implemented properly, EOS can transform many businesses from disjointed and difficult to cohesive and exciting. In Gino Wickman's book *Traction*, entrepreneurs can learn how to start with *who* by ensuring the right people are in the right seats. They can also start with *who* by understanding their "three uniques" that drive customer interest and adoption. EOS offers a clear road map to success, but several EOS Implementers agree it's not all inclusive. There are always additional considerations and tools that can ensure ultimate success.

Dave Borland became an EOS Implementer after founding three successful start-ups. He has since used the EOS People Analyzer for over six hundred sessions and discovered that it's an amazing tool; however, he believes the process of people selection could benefit from additional unbiased data. "An executive may give a thumbs-up for an employee when evaluating them with the People Analyzer because they don't want to hurt anyone's feelings," says Borland. "I try to help them see that getting to the right *who* is foundationally important. Adding more data to the equation to make better people decisions can help remove the bias that could lead to keeping the wrong people in the wrong seats."

Pat Atwal is also an EOS Implementer. She helps clients use an Accountability Chart to ensure the wrong people don't remain on the bus. "Managers should discuss any concerns with employees across three separate meetings," says Atwal. "Managers should be prepared to show three examples of where an employee is not meeting their accountability requirements. They should be given thirty days to correct any issues, and if they are still not measuring up, another final thirty days to turn things around. If there are still too many issues, it may be time to let them go."

Rob Drynan launched a nonprofit that grew by 400 percent and won several awards before he switched tracks and became an EOS Implementer. He notes that while the EOS framework is exceptionally powerful and can be life-changing, it is a foundational program that can benefit from additional layers. "Once an organization has determined their three uniques," says Drynan, "they might benefit from more advanced tactics and strategies to improve sales messaging. There may be additional tools that could help propel them forward. EOS provides an excellent foundation. It's the cake atop which you can add almost any flavor of icing you like."

Aaron Purkeypile launched his career with Deloitte in Omaha, Nebraska, before reading the book *Traction*. He later found his passion and purpose as an EOS Implementer. He has worked with several clients who've used various candidate-assessment tools to ensure they place the right people in the right seats. "Some of my clients have invested in legacy solutions such as Myers-Briggs or DISC, which were invented more than eighty years ago," says Purkeypile. "Others have used some that are perhaps a decade or two old, such as Kolbe or Culture Index. These can all be helpful, but they can also be expensive and complex. Some tests take a long time to complete, so some candidates, especially the top ones with several options available, may not finish them. Difficult, lengthy, or confusing tests might also result in a less than favorable candidate experience."

Purkeypile became a board advisor for RemotelyMe and recommends this visual neuroscience-based solution, as it can be less complex, more affordable, and offer more accuracy than text-based assessments.

After managing eleven stores for Walmart, Evan Blumenthal helped grow his family's business revenue by over $25 million before finding EOS. He became an Implementer and now helps clients pave their way to more revenue and freedom. Blumenthal notes that most of his clients are small firms and don't have a dedicated human resources person, let alone an entire team. "For most of my clients, HR is a part-time function for someone in the organization," says Blumenthal. "They can't afford sophisticated HR information systems, applicant tracking systems, or costly candidate-assessment solutions. They also can't afford LinkedIn Recruiter, which can be quite expensive."

Blumenthal says his clients would like to be more proactive in finding candidates, given that the best ones are likely not looking for new jobs. However, finding the time and tools to do this can be a challenge. Blumenthal is also a RemotelyMe board advisor and recommends the company's ChatGEM.ai solution, as it's effective and inexpensive.

"A part-time HR person can use LinkedIn Sales Navigator at an affordable cost to search for candidates. Then, use the RemotelyMe LinkedIn AI app to extract candidate data and analyze it. ChatGEM.ai automatically creates optimal prompts for an included ChatGPT copy creator that crafts candidate email messages in seconds."

Justin Mink decided to become an EOS Implementer after starting a music marketing company in Dallas, Texas. He understands that change can be difficult, but it's necessary to achieve your long-range goals. "EOS Implementers help firms create one-, three-, and ten-year plans to ensure everyone understands the vision and is aligned with the goals of the company," says Mink. "You should pick a model and stick with it. I believe EOS is the best model, and 150,000 companies apparently agree, but it's not the only one available."

Mink also decided to become a RemotelyMe board advisor to help his clients improve their recruiting, sales, and marketing success.

Julie Markee started her first business at eleven years of age. While she loved being an entrepreneur, she pursued a career as a chemical engineer, which relied heavily upon processes. Attracted by the simplistic power of the EOS process, she later became an Implementer. Determining the "three uniques" can be a giant step in the right direction, but her clients often still face a few marketing challenges. "They still need to clearly define how they differentiate from competitors," says Markee. "They need to ask why their customers and target markets will care about or resonate with their three uniques. They must tell a proper story and understand that they are not the hero of the story, the customer is the hero."

Justin Cook was an entrepreneur in Nashville, Tennessee, before he became an EOS Implementer. He agrees that companies should have a single business operating system, such as EOS, but he understands that many sales teams may use a variety of sales frameworks such as Sandler, Miller Heiman, or *The Challenger Sale*. "It may be difficult to force your sales team to adopt a single way of selling," says Cook. "Seasoned sales professionals may be reluctant to move away from what's helped them be successful. It might be better to find solutions that overlay atop these frameworks to create unity rather than rip and replace."

Tim Tannert was a pharmacist before he became an EOS Implementer. He often sees the number one problem with clients as attracting and retaining the right and best talent. "Many of my clients may be reluctant to ask 'bad apples' to leave," says Tannert. "They may be concerned about losing that person's capability or placing stress on others to do the work until a replacement is hired. I ask them to envision what their future might look like without this person. Is this individual causing disruption? If they stay, will others feel compelled to leave? The short term without them might be painful, but the long term with them might be worse."

Andrew Stevens played trumpet in the British army for several years before joining the sales and marketing team for a Silicon Valley technology firm. He experienced leadership chaos before reading the book *Traction* and later became an EOS Implementer. He now has sixteen EOS clients that are moving toward reduced stress while increasing revenue. "Almost all my clients benefited greatly by clearly defining their three uniques." says Stevens. "However, almost all still struggle with implementing effective product marketing strategies, messaging, and sales enablement. They can certainly benefit from techniques and tools that augment EOS in these areas."

Andrea Young was a corporate executive with the Coca-Cola corporation for many years before she decided to help smaller firms implement EOS. Prior to adopting EOS, many of her clients were frustrated and unprofitable, lacked control, and did not have healthy cultures. "EOS has helped my clients take the mystery out of how they need to operate," says Young. "They can now invest more time and energy into what they do best."

Young admonishes her clients to become crystal clear on people. While they all use the People Analyzer, some do supplement this with candidate-assessment solutions such as Kolbe, Culture Index, Hogan, or RemotelyMe. These tools can help firms use data to remove bias and validate decisions.

Joel Swanson, an EOS Implementer who views his role as more of a teacher, facilitator, and business coach, says, "You can do whatever you want or you can get whatever you want. You can't do both. You need to pick one or the other."

***

Most of us have heard the famous quote attributed to Albert Einstein: "The definition of insanity is doing the same thing over and over and expecting different results."

If we're not getting what we want from our professional or personal lives, perhaps it's time to make a change.

***

By now, you may be feeling a bit overwhelmed. We've covered a lot of ground, and some of it might be confusing. Let's simplify all we've learned down to a few steps that correspond to the three-act play so we can easily put the concepts in this book into practice. We'll take a page from Gino Wickman's book *Traction* to help smooth our path.

As we now know, the EOS model recommends determining your firm's core values. If you work for an established organization, these values may already be defined. If not, it may be difficult to persuade anyone to do anything if you don't know why you want them to do it. So, a core value exercise may be valuable. But…let's take the core value process a step further.

Start With Why and 4MAT alignment

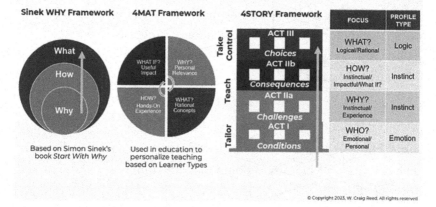

© Copyright 2023, W. Craig Reed. All rights reserved.

In the above graphic, we can again see how the 4STORY framework aligns with Sinek's *Start with Why* and the 4MAT framework used in educational circles. Recall that in Act I we start with the first floor, or building story, and go upward from there. Let's take a deeper dive into this process from two perspectives, both from the prospect (sales and marketing) perspective and from the people (recruiting and employee) perspective.

STORY I/ACT I: *WHO ARE YOU AND WHO ARE YOUR TARGET CUSTOMERS (OR CANDIDATES)?*

Let's say you have or want to have six core values. Edit or create them such that you have two core values for each act in a three-act play. If possible, create two core values that are more emotional, two that are instinctual, and two logical. For example, let's say your six values are trust, courage, intelligence, teamwork, analytics, and empathy. You might align your values as such:

Act I: empathy, teamwork

Act II: courage, trust

Act III: intelligence, analytics

Do we see how these line up? In Act I, we have the more emotional values of empathy and teamwork. In Act II, our instinctual values are courage and trust. Finally, in Act III, intelligence and analytics are obviously logical values. When placed in the proper order, they tell the *story* of who you are as a company. Now you can better attract and retain the right people and prospects.

Recall our previous discussion about ideal customer profiles, or ICPs? ICP can also stand for ideal candidate profiles on the recruiting side of the fence. You can certainly dive into the weeds and complicate this process with mounds of research data, but it does not need to be that complex. Let's again use the three-act play to simplify this. As an example, let's say you're a real estate firm catering to middle class individuals seeking median- to high-priced homes. Your story might be:

> Act I: Our ideal customers want a life of comfort and simplicity in quiet neighborhoods.
>
> Act II: Our ideal customers want safe neighborhoods in school districts known for excellence.
>
> Act III: Our ideal customers want affordable homes with high quality and elegance.

You can turn the above into six keywords as follows:

> Act I: comfort, simplicity
>
> Act II: safety, excellence
>
> Act III: affordability, elegance

The above exercise might seem like it narrows your scope, and therefore you'll miss out on several opportunities, but just the opposite is true. It's hard to say no to business, but sometimes that's the best strategy. Also, as prescribed by the EOS model, it's less about turning down business as it is about focusing on the *right* business. Rather than spend time and dollars marketing to the wrong prospects, laser focus on the ones you can service the best. The above profile can be further refined using traditional ICP definitions such as, "We target clients seeking homes less than fifteen years old to ensure lower cost of ownership and a life of ease." When you focus on who your best clients might be, you can eventually gain a reputation as the best choice for those types. For example, Nordstrom knows exactly who they want to walk through their doors, don't they?

The above approach can also be used by recruiters to target ideal candidates. Simply create similar statements such as, "Our ideal candidates want to work for a firm that values empathy and teamwork." Be sure to create three such statements that are emotional, instinctual, and logical.

Next, we need to speak to our ICs—ideal customers or candidates. To do so, we should create a messaging guide, which most product marketers use for each product and the company as a whole. This ensures consistency across all collateral, web pages, sales tools, and so on. Delving into the structure of a messaging guide is beyond the scope of this book, but you can find an excellent framework to use by visiting RemotelyMe.com/consulting.

For now, we'll keep it simple by focusing on how to use the 4STORY format to craft basic messaging. Starting with the first story, or floor, if we currently have customers, we should analyze them to determine similarities. The same can be done with employees by analyzing our top performers. Perhaps they're all seven-foot basketball players, in which case they're easy to find but hard to see eye to eye. Okay, all kidding aside, marketers call this a persona exercise. Given that we all think in threes, from an ideal customer perspective, I recommend using only three personas.

For example, with a B2B company, you might have an influencer, evaluator, and decision-maker. Influencers rarely make decisions but can help open doors and provide valuable company information. Evaluators can make decisions, typically related to whether a solution is adequate or worthy of further investigation or a trial, but usually do not have the final say. Decision-makers, obviously, make final decisions but may be strongly influenced by influencers and evaluators. Determining which titles or roles fall into each of these categories is a good start, but we should go further. We should seek to understand what attributes and brain wiring are optimal for our ideal customer profile. One of the best and easiest ways to do this is by using the RemotelyMe browser app that extracts all relevant data from someone's LinkedIn page and then parses the data. The information is placed into separate fields for About, Skills, Interests, Experience, Recommendations, etc. Once in the system, the app uses AI and neuroscience to analyze everything to determine one of nine likely profile types (e.g., ambitious, helpful, logical, etc.). You can then begin to see what attributes, soft skills, and so on relate to your ideal customers. Now you can use the app to extract the same data from prospects and match that against your ideal customers.

The above approach can also be used for recruiting. For each position open in your firm, determine if the role is more influencer, evaluator, or decision-maker. For example, an individual contributor might be an influencer, and a director and above might be considered an evaluator or decision-maker. The RemotelyMe app can also help determine optimal attributes and soft skills for top performers. For example, a leading real estate firm had very high turnover—over 85 percent of new Realtors were failing or quitting within eighteen months. They assessed their top performers and discovered that 90 percent fell into three distinct "brain wiring" categories with similar attributes and soft skills. Going forward, they were able to assess candidates against this top performer data to help guide them toward the right careers. Perhaps not as Realtors but instead in other roles at the company where they were more likely to thrive. This approach can help save hundreds of hours and hundreds of thousands of dollars for recruiting, onboarding, training, and more.

Now that we know *who* we're trying to sell, we need to create a story arc. This is simply a circular arrow starting from where they are in Act I to where they want to be in Act III. For example, our homebuyers might already perceive that they have reasonable comfort and simplicity where they are (Act I). However, something (perhaps a nudge from us) has motivated them to explore moving out of their comfort zone. The arc takes them from moderate comfort to affordable elegance that includes even more comfort and simplicity combined with safety and excellence. This brings together several persuasive elements:

- Emotional, instinctual, and logical appeals (Aristotle's Persuasion Model)
- Contrasts and the power of three
- Storytelling (three-act play)

Our next step is to determine what might motivate our ideal customers to move out of Kansas and explore a new neighborhood by understanding where they are and why they may want to change. We again use our three-act play to list potential customer motivators. In Act I, ask the question: For our ideal customers, where is Kansas? For example, if we're a Realtor, our market focus (from our exercise above) is on nice neighborhoods with excellent school districts. Therefore, what might motivate ideal customers to move to these types of homes? Perhaps individuals now living in less elegant neighborhoods looking for a change? Or even more likely, those in smaller houses wanting to take a step up from their current areas.

> Act I: Our ideal customers are affluent, in midlevel careers, and living in moderate but not elegant areas.
>
> Act II: Our ideal customers were recently promoted, started a family, etc., and are motivated to change.
>
> Act III: Our ideal customers are successful, ego-driven, and appreciate quality.

It's important to note that ego-driven and egotistical are not the same. Ego-driven is usually considered healthy and refers to individuals who take pride in their accomplishments or titles. They may be quite humble, but they are driven to perform at their best. They may also want the best for their families, including a nice new house. With a pool. And a wicked cool BBQ island so they can keep up with their old neighbor, Mr. Jones.

Recruiters can also use this to understand candidate motivators. Where are ideal candidates now along their career path? If you're looking for a director role, perhaps targeting senior managers at competitive firms might be ideal.

Once we've identified who we're targeting and why they may want to listen, we need to figure out how to reach them.

STORY II/ACT IIA: HOW WILL YOU REACH YOUR ICP?

We can also use the three-act play to determine how to find and begin to motivate our ideal customers. Simply create three more lines labeled Act I, II, and III as shown below. Your statements and keywords might be:

> Act I: Our ideal customers have LinkedIn profiles and are reasonably sociable.
>
> Act II: Our ideal customers don't like cold calls or spam and prefer low-risk referrals.
>
> Act III: Our ideal customers like nicer restaurants, shops, etc., that offer affordable quality.

Our six keywords might be:

> Act I: LinkedIn, sociable
>
> Act II: referrals, low-risk
>
> Act III: affordable, quality

Once we've completed this exercise, we can begin to see how best to reach our ideal customers. The same can be done for our ideal candidates. We should use more efficient and affordable rifle shots rather than expensive and wasteful shotgun blasts. For example, if our ideal customers or candidates have LinkedIn profiles, we'll want to reach them on this platform. We might consider using LinkedIn Sales Navigator, which allows us to do sophisticated searches that might include a new career change, promotion, or recent move to a new area (they could still be renting). For recruiters, there's LinkedIn Recruiter, but this can be expensive for many firms. Sales Navigator is significantly less cost per month and uses the same database as Recruiter—so you're essentially reaching the same audience. Once you've completed a search, using the RemotelyMe app lets you extract and analyze the data with a single click.

If your ideal customers are sociable, which LinkedIn groups might they prefer? Are there local areas they might often visit, such as a dog park or museum (where you might advertise)? Since they don't like cold calls or spam, can you consider a way to Connect on LinkedIn and then send Messages (instead of costly InMail)? For example, RemotelyMe lets you leverage their exclusive Leaders Forum group. When you use their LinkedIn Profiling app, you can invite prospects or candidates to this group as a way to get them to Connect.

If your ideal customers or candidates prefer quality but affordable restaurants and stores, can you advertise there? Ask owners if you can pay to have flyers on their counters. A brainstorming exercise with your team can help uncover additional ICP insights and ideas, and once you have a list of where and how to find prospects and candidates, it's time to make an initial connection. We need to do this in the right way, preferably by personalizing our messages, to ensure response.

Many marketers create email or message cadences using numerous variations that may appeal to specific personas—such as decision-makers. Recruiters often do something similar. One organization I've worked with had nine hundred templates for their talent acquisition team, which was confusing and time consuming. Even when a firm has templates, many sales or recruiting professionals may spend a half hour analyzing someone's LinkedIn profile, résumé, or other information to extract key data to use so they can personalize messages. Fortunately, artificial intelligence can simplify this task.

We've all heard of ChatGPT, right? It's a game changer from a firm called OpenAI, but it can also be frustrating. You need to know exactly how to instruct AI to gain the best results. Many complain that it takes more time to tell ChatGPT and similar AI tools how to do something correctly than it does to do it yourself. The RemotelyMe app can solve this problem by using extracted LinkedIn data and AI profiling analysis to automatically create ChatGPT prompts. All you need to do is copy and paste the recommended prompts into the included copy creator and within seconds you have a well-written personalized email or message that includes a prospect's LinkedIn info, such as skills and interests, as well as profile keywords and the proper tone that will resonate with the prospect or candidate and increase response rates. For recruiters, the same can be done to write compelling job descriptions.

Assuming your prospect or candidate does respond, how should you reply? In this act, we need to probe for concerns, issues, problems, and so forth. We need to understand where it hurts but also inform and teach them about potential pains they may not know about. For example, if a real estate prospect is the type who's motivated by safety and security, you might inform them about a recent increase in the crime rate for their area. This can inject a new concern that might motivate them to move.

We can use the three-act play to craft questions that will help us probe for concerns and teach prospects or candidates about unknown problems. Here's an example we might create for real estate prospects:

> Act I: With your current home, based on your likes and dislikes, why might you stay or consider moving?

> Act II: You're in a high fire zone and fires are increasing. Why might this be a concern for you?

> Act III: If your family is growing, why might you be worried about the low school ratings in your area?

Obviously, similar questions can be written for other industries and for recruiting. For example, if you're in high tech you might ask: "If one of your ancient servers blows up and starts a fire that burns down your data center, will you get fired?"

That one has always worked well for me.

On a side note, we used the word "why" in each of the examples above. Why might this align with Sinek's *Start with Why* model?

STORY III/ACT IIB: HOW WILL YOU MOTIVATE YOUR ICP?

Across dozens of executive consulting projects I've been involved with, I've often seen professional salespersons pounce on prospects after they've expressed a concern or two. Being zealous is desirable, but the most successful pros pull back on the reins before delivering solution information that can solve someone's problems. They first raise the stakes in the game.

Recall from our storytelling chapters that the best stories escalate tension, especially in Act II, and even more so in Act IIb. We need to do the same with prospects or candidates. Once a few concerns have been determined, we need to probe and teach for consequences of inaction or wrong action. Remember, our biggest competitor is Mr. Do Nothing.

Here are some question examples we can use to do this. Note how they align with the concern questions we previously asked (using the real estate example).

> Act I: If you stay in a home where you have so many dislikes, how might this impact your relationship with your family? How might this impact your health?

> Act II: If you remain in a fire hazard area, how bad might it be if you lost everything in a fire?

> Act III: If your children are forced to attend schools with low ratings, how might that impact their ability to apply for the best colleges?

Again, similar questions can be asked of candidates, such as, "If you stay working for that crappy company you're with, will all your colleagues think you're a moron?" Okay, you might want to tone it down a bit, but you get the idea. Notice how we've used the word "how" in the examples above? This, of course, aligns with Sinek's *Start with Why*.

Once we've scared the crap out of our prospects or candidates, we can become more logical and amaze them with cool facts and figures.

STORY IV/ACT III: WHAT WILL YOU DO TO CONVINCE YOUR ICP?

Here's your first test question: In Act III, should we be more emotional, instinctual, or logical? If you answered emotional or instinctual, you should hang your head in shame and reread this book from the beginning. For those who answered logical, congratulations—you can now record a TikTok video of yourself doing a happy dance.

Here's your second test question: What does our logical brain prefer, fancy images or factual text? Okay that was a no-brainer, every pun intended. To refresh, we've determined who our ideal customers or candidates might be. We've figured out how to find them, reach them, scare them, and motivate them. Now, we need to convince them with logical data. Here are some questions we might ask, again aligning with our real estate example:

> Act I: What if you could afford to move to a new home with a number of the features you'd like and low total cost of ownership?
>
> Act II: What if your new home was located in a safe non-fire hazard zone that helped reduce the cost of your home insurance by 15 percent?
>
> Act III: What if your children could attend the best schools with the highest ratings that provided a 20 percent higher probability of getting accepted to the best colleges?

Using the term "what if" is an old sales approach that's worked well across many decades, and it also aligns with Sinek's *Start with Why*. More importantly, we use facts and figures throughout to appeal to the logical brain. Doing this brings us home to Kansas where our prospects, perhaps literally, learn that there's no place like home. In this case, a *new* home by using us as their trusty Realtor.

To recap, implementing the *Start with Who* principles is as easy as telling a good story. That's really all you need to remember. Start with Act I, go to Act II, end with Act III. Emotional, instinctual, logical. If you'd like a catchy tune to help with remembering this, think of "Old MacDonald." Surely you recall this one from childhood? Old MacDonald had a cow, e-i-e-i-o? In this case, use the tune to sing e-i-e-i-*l*, as in emotional, instinctual, logical. Now you'll never be able to get this song out of your head. It will haunt you forever, and you're welcome.

CONCLUSIONS

- ICP stands for "I can pick the ideal customer profiles," such as people who like chocolate.
- Your ideal customers live in crappy homes.
- Since Old MacDonald had a farm, your ideal customers like steaks.

CHAPTER 20
INSIDE JOB

*"Some people see things that are and ask, 'Why?'
Some people dream of things that never were
and ask, 'Why not?' Some people have to go to
work and don't have time for all that."*
—George Carlin

Selling, marketing, and recruiting...is an inside job.

A few decades ago, at the beginning of my career, I stepped into the shoes of a national sales manager position for a technology firm in San Diego, California. I was filled with equal parts pride, excitement, and trepidation. About a year into the job, I started to hate my boss. His name was Ron, and I thought he was a jerk. He had a tight mustache and a smug scowl and appeared to take great pleasure in demeaning subordinates, most especially me. I worked my tail off for Ron. I did everything he asked and more. I burned the midnight oil, crossed all my T's, and shined my shoes to polished perfection.

Then I had my first performance review. Even though I thought my team's sales quota was way too high, we had at least come close to hitting it. Even so, he gave me mediocre marks and said, "I don't have any major issues with you, except that your tie, and your smile, are always out of alignment."

All I heard was that my tie was askew. I felt like saying, "My tie is askew? Dang, if only I'd known. I feel so...embarrassed. Should I prepare myself for the firing squad?"

I walked out of Ron's office in shock. Here I thought I'd done everything right, including closing far more deals than my predecessor. I had been the perfect little soldier and yet had been given average marks and branded as a loser for a fashion faux pas.

Determined, I doubled down. I pushed my team to double their performance and put in twice as many hours. I even bought new ties and made sure they were perfectly straight. Months passed, and the results came in. My team and I still hadn't quite hit our quota, but thanks to the deals we had closed, our division had outperformed all the others and broke quite a few company sales records. I felt proud. Now, finally, I was certain I'd receive the high marks I deserved and perhaps even a big raise. Most importantly, I was sure I'd get a major award at the company's next event.

During the awards ceremony, I squirmed in my seat. My palms were sweaty, and my heart pounded so hard that my new ties bounced on my chest. I just knew they were going to call my name at any moment. I imagined myself basking in the limelight, the cameras flashing, the crowd cheering, the smiles, the handshakes, the pats on the back.

The CEO stood. I swallowed hard. He praised our division for stellar results, for the records we'd broken, and the hard work we'd displayed.

By now my smile was so wide you could have parked a Hummer on my tongue. The CEO held up a plaque. In excited anticipation, I rose from my seat. I heard him call a name. It wasn't mine. Ron stood. With a beaming smile on his smug face, he stepped toward the podium and accepted the highest award the company had ever given an employee.

Devastated, I slumped in my seat. My heart sank so low in my chest that it almost touched my sour gut. It was all I could do to hold back the tears. I felt a slap on my back and heard a colleague say, "Suck it up, buddy. Maybe next time."

If I'd hated my boss before, I despised him now. No longer motivated to perform, resigned to a state of depression, I suited up and showed up but had little desire to sell more than what was needed to keep my job. I secretly complained about my boss to peers and relived my pain over and over again. I reveled in playing the victim and used my pitiful pout to gain favors and help from others. Why not? I should at least get something for being so unfairly treated.

One day Ron called me into his office. He said nothing as I sat in the uncomfortable chair in front of his desk for what felt like an eternity. Finally, he spoke and asked me if something was wrong. I lied and said everything was fine. He didn't buy it and probed some more. After twenty questions and twenty minutes, I finally opened up and admitted that I had felt slighted at the awards ceremony.

He smiled and asked me one question: "Why did you choose your profession?"

Surprised by this question, I wasn't sure how to respond. I wasn't married at the time, so "to provide for my family" would have been an inaccurate answer. I said, "To be successful, I guess."

"Define success," Ron asked.

I straightened my already straight tie. "To achieve my goals."

"What are your goals?"

Being goal oriented, I spewed out the usual quantitative figures.

Ron leaned forward, and then threw me a curveball. "Okay, those are good professional goals, but what are your personal goals? What's your purpose and passion in life?"

The question confused me. "My purpose and passion? I'm not sure what you mean."

"All of your goals are career oriented. I get that you want to be the greatest sales manager on earth, but what else do you want to be?"

"What else?"

"What about being the greatest son, brother, husband, father, person, leader, mentor? Do any of these things matter to you?"

I almost got mad. "Of course they do! I'm not married yet, but sure, someday I want to be a good husband and father, and of course I want to be a great leader."

"What about just being a good person who truly cares about others and how they feel?"

Heat rose from under my collar. "Why do you think I'm not a good person?"

"I never said you weren't. Why do you think you are?"

"I give to charities, and I care when other people are hurting or depressed. I'm not unfeeling."

Ron pulled out a file. I recognized the folder. It contained information on my largest customer.

"Tell me about Ted."

"Ted?"

"Ted. He's the decision-maker for your biggest account. Who is he? What's he like? What's his favorite sports team? Is he married? What's his wife's name? Children's names? Hobbies? What's his personality?"

I was stumped. I had to admit that I knew only a fraction of the answers.

Then Ron asked, "Who's on your team here at our firm, and what do you know about them?"

I blinked and said nothing.

Ron continued, "Who are all the people in this company who directly or indirectly make it possible for you to succeed? Salespersons, admins, telemarketing, shipping, legal, finance, HR, support, channels, you name it. How many of them do you know personally, know anything about, talk to regularly, are grateful for, or who hear you say 'thank you' on a frequent basis?"

I lowered my head and remained silent.

When I finally raised my chin, Ron locked his eyes with mine. "Do you recall when I said your tie and your smile were out of alignment?"

I nodded, not sure where this was going.

"I didn't mean it literally. Your techniques, acumen, and product knowledge are flawless, but you don't truly connect with your customers, subordinates, peers, or colleagues on a deep personal level. Maybe you haven't won any awards because you're leading with your head and not your heart."

Stunned, I rose from my seat and walked out of his office. At first, the space between my ears contained only silent arguments. I tried to convince myself that Ron was completely wrong. Of course I cared about my customers and colleagues. How could he intimate that I didn't?

A few days later, after I calmed down, I realized what he'd meant about my tie and smile being out of alignment.

My head was in the game, but my heart was not. I had every product specification and company fact memorized. I had read leadership books, attended management training classes, and knew all the facts about leading. But if I was truly honest with myself, I had no idea *who* most of my customers really were. I smiled in their presence, but it wasn't genuine. I wasn't uncaring, but I saw most of my customers as puppets with strings that I should pull to hit my numbers and gain big commission checks.

I also had to admit that I knew very few of the dozens of people who empowered me to do my job. I had rarely connected with them and knew next to nothing about them. I had not frequently been grateful for them, nor had I often thanked them for their help. How could I be a great leader if I had no idea *who* I was leading?

In that moment of clarity, I realized that more often than not, my leadership style was like a heartless tin man. I realized that becoming the greatest leader on earth should no longer be my goal. Instead, it was time to become the greatest *person* I could be. In doing so, I would begin to understand my true purpose and passion in life, and become the greatest leader I was meant to be.

Perhaps the above is a bit too "touchy-feely" for some, but this may be the most important success principle you will ever hear: Selling is an inside job. So is marketing or recruiting. So is living. All of us spend most of our lives focused outwardly. We point a finger without seeing three fingers pointed back. As we know, Simon Sinek espouses a process flow that begins with Why, followed by How and then What. He admonishes that the best companies and leaders start with Why they are offering a product or service or idea before explaining How they offer these. What they offer is tertiary. As outlined in this book, I believe there's a fourth W that comes before Why.

Who.

We must first know *who* may want to do business with us, be inspired by us, or want to work for us. Also, the Who and the Why must be selfless. The hero of our story is not *us*, it's *them*. Passion and purpose must pervade every aspect of our Who and Why, or else our ties and our smiles will remain out of alignment. We must care about our target customers or candidates, our perfect personas, our prospects and partners, like we care about our families. This requires understanding the Principle of Familiarity.

The word "familiarity" has its roots in the Latin word *familia*, which, as it sounds, refers to "family." Most of us are familiar with and therefore usually bond with our immediate family. While we might squabble occasionally with our siblings and parents, we're usually far more motivated to help our brother or sister than we are to help a complete stranger. It's not that we lack any feelings for strangers, but we have acquired a level of familiarity and therefore a close bond with family members we love, so they will always take precedence. This is just human nature. We therefore must learn how to treat others, including those we are privileged to lead, work with, or connect with in a business setting, as if they are close family. I realize that for some of us, there are family members we can't stand, but for most of us, there are those who mean the world to us. We need to treat everyone in our life, even those we don't like, with love and respect regardless of how they treat us. We can best accomplish this by creating an emotional bond that connects our limbic brain with theirs in a meaningful way. This does not start with them; it starts with us.

Before we can truly connect with others and craft messaging, sales scripts, collateral, sales plays, emails, LinkedIn messages, and everything else that motivates our prospects or candidates to take action, we must first align our ties and our smiles. I realize that few men wear ties anymore, and most women have never worn them, but metaphorically I'm referring to our inward appearance, not outward.

We need to first spend some time determining and examining our personal and professional passion and purpose. To do so, we must affirm that it's our right, and our responsibility—not someone else's—to determine our true purpose in life. All of us have needs, personally and professionally, and to enjoy a happy, healthy, and productive life, these needs must be understood and met in an appropriate way.

To determine our most important needs, we must first understand our core beliefs. These beliefs, and their underlying values, dictate our needs. For example, if our belief is that it's our responsibility to nurture and care for our families, one of our needs may be income. That means we probably need a job or business. But what kind of job? If our list of beliefs does not include the need for superficial, ego-gratifying luxuries (as fun and desirable as these may be), then do we really need that high-paying yet highly stressful career that keeps us away from home? Do we really need that brand-new and expensive car, or does that desire stem from an antiquated and unhealthy belief that our neighbors and friends will think less of us if we drive something modest?

This viewpoint may seem contrary to the "you can have it all" philosophies espoused by many other self-help books or programs. These authors or well-meaning advisors may say we must all set lofty goals and focus on pictures of the fancy house or car we desire. If we do so, the universe will magically make them appear just as we imagined. This may be true, but how often have we focused on the "desire of our hearts," only to discover that it was not at all what we really wanted—or needed? Perhaps we fixated on that big house by convincing ourselves we needed it to provide for our families. Years later, the "universe" or God or hard work or whatever we believe in miraculously granted us our wish.

As we stood in our mansion with the spiral staircase and manicured lawn and massive pool, we patted ourselves on the back for attaining our dream. It all came true, just as we envisioned, yet we are not smiling. Our grand house is empty because our spouse divorced us and took the kids. We worked so hard that we forgot about them. The medical report in our pocket says we have only six months to live. We stressed so hard we failed to take care of ourselves, and a fatal illness caught us unaware.

How often have we heard "careful what you wish for"?

Maybe it's better not to wish or pray for specific outcomes, lest our limited knowledge of the future prevent us from fulfilling the destiny we are meant to have. Perhaps we should ask only for the wisdom to discern what is right and best for us today—each day—that will lead us to a life filled with joy and abundance.

ANCIENT TAR

In ancient times, the Sumerians used the word "NAM.TAR" to depict one's fate. Namtar was a mythical god who dwelled in the underworld and brought forth evil, pestilence, and disease that Sumerians thought of as the "fate of the gods." More importantly, Namtar acted as a herald or messenger of fates beyond one's control.

Today, we often bemoan our fate and wonder why bad things happen to good people...like us. We question what we did to "deserve this fate." We forget that we probably asked for it when we prayed for, hoped for, or asked the Universe or God or whatever we believe in for an outcome.

We wanted to be healthier, so why did we get sick? To develop an immunity. We wanted to be richer, so why did we get hammered in the stock market? To teach us how to invest better. We wanted to reach that goal at work, so why did our team fail? So we'd learn how to work smarter as a team and succeed in the future.

Be careful what you wish for. If you're not prepared to take the bad as a stepping stone to reach the good, then be content with where you are. If you're not content with where you are, the Sumerians used another word called "TAR."

This word means destiny. It literally means to cut or break, as in altering one's future path. TAR describes a predetermined course that can be changed by what we do...or think. For the Sumerians, TAR began in the heavens with the preordained path of the planets and arrangement of the universe. However, our TAR can only be altered by changing what *can* and *should* be changed.

Perhaps this is what inspired the saying by Reinhold Niebuhr:

> "Grant me the serenity to accept the things I cannot change, Courage to change the things I can."

As you embark upon or continue your journey toward becoming the best and most successful sales, marketing, or human resources professional in the universe, I encourage you to take a moment to apply the power of three and list your top three desires in life. What is your true passion and purpose? Beyond temporal riches and accolades, *who* are you and *why* are you really here? Once you know this to the depths of your soul, *how* will you act going forward and *what* will you do to attain your life's desires?

Only after you've answered these questions for yourself can you successfully engage with and persuade others, including your prospects, colleagues, and subordinates. Until then, you will be nothing more than another annoying cold call, ignored advertisement, or failed business leader.

For more information on how to implement the *Start with Who* and 4STORY concepts outlined in this book as well as discover how the LinkedIn Profiling App can improve your ability to understand and motivate prospects, please email admin@remotelyme.com or visit RemotelyMe.com/consulting.

SOURCES

American Psychological Association (2018). "Personality." Retrieved from http://www.apa.org/topics/personality/.

Ariely, D., & Berns, G. S. (2010). "Neuromarketing: The hope and hype of neuroimaging in business." *Nature Reviews Neuroscience* 11(4), 284–292. doi:10.1038/nrn2795.

Aristotle (1992). *The Art of Rhetoric* (1st ed.). London, UK: Penguin.

Barna Group (2015). "The different impact of good and bad leadership." Retrieved from https://www.barna.com/research/the-different-impact-of-good-and-bad-leadership/.

Barsade, S. G., & Gibson, D. E. (2007). "Why does affect matter in organizations?" *Academy of Management Perspectives* 21(1): 36–59.

Bergland, C. (May 9, 2015). "How do your genes influence levels of emotional sensitivity?" *Psychology Today*. Retrieved from https://www.psychologytoday.com/us/blog/the-athletes-way/201505/how-do-your-genes-influence-levels-emotional-sensitivity.

Boal, K. B., & Hooijberg, R. (2001). "Strategic leadership research: Moving on." *The Leadership Quarterly* 11(4): 515–549.

Boaz, N., & Fox, E. (March 2014). "Change leader, change thyself." *McKinsey Quarterly*.

Boushey, H., & Glynn, S. (November 16, 2012). "There Are Significant Business Costs to Replacing Employees." The Center for American Progress. Retrieved from https://www.americanprogress.org/article/there-are-significant-business-costs-to-replacing-employees/.

Boyatzis, R. (January 2011). "Neuroscience and Leadership: The Promise of Insights." *The Kensho Search Advantage*. Retrieved from https://www.researchgate.net/publication/265068320_Neuroscience_and_Leadership_The_Promise_of_Insights.

Braverman, E. (2004). *The Edge Effect.* New York: Sterling Publishing Co., Inc., 18–26.

British Broadcasting Corporation (November 10, 2009). "Bad bosses 'force staff to quit.'" BBC News. http://news.bbc.co.uk/2/hi/business/8352389.stm.

Brown, A., & Bartram, D. (June 2005). "Relationships between OPQ and Enneagram types." SHL Group, Version 1.3.

Cacioppo, J. T., Berntson, G. G., & Nusbaum, H. C. (2008). "Neuroimaging as a new tool in the toolbox of psychological science." *Current Directions in Psychological Science* 17(2): 62–67.

Chong, B. (June 28, 2017). "Tasks & relationships." PennState. Retrieved from https://sites.psu.edu/leadership/2017/06/28/tasks-relationships/.

Clear, J. (April 29, 2014). "Use the 'Eisenhower box' to stop wasting time and be more productive." *Entrepreneur*. Retrieved from https://www.entrepreneur.com/article/233054.

Edwards, S. (May 2005). "The amygdala: The body's alarm circuit." The Dana Foundation. Retrieved from https://dnalc.cshl.edu/view/822-The-Amygdala-the-Body-s-Alarm-Circuit.html.

Fatemi, F. (September 28, 2016). "The True Cost of a Bad Hire—It's More Than You Think." *Forbes*. https://www.forbes.com/sites/falonfatemi/2016/09/28/the-true-cost-of-a-bad-hire-its-more-than-you-think/?sh=428e942a4aa4.

Forbes Staff (May 11, 2015). "The World's Largest Tech Companies." *Forbes*. https://www.forbes.com/pictures/fjlj45fkfh/9-hp/?sh=6182b0bb119a.

Fresco, G. (October 12, 2015). "Neuroscience of selling." Adaptive Neuroscience Research Institute. Retrieved from http://adaptive-neuroscience.com/2015/10/12/neuroscience-of-selling/.

Friedman, C. (September 20, 2022). "The Power of Data Storytelling." St. Charles Consulting Group. Retrieved from https://stccg.com/the-power-of-data-storytelling/.

Gallup (2013). "State of the Global Workplace: 2023 Report." Retrieved from https://www.gallup.com/workplace/349484/state-of-the-global-workplace.aspx.

Gill, C. (1983). "The question of character-development: Plutarch and Tacitus." *The Classical Quarterly* 33(2): 469-487. doi:10.1017/S0009838800034741.

Goldberg, Lewis R. (1992). "The development of markers for the Big-Five factor structure." *Psychological Assessment* 4(1): 26–42. http://dx.doi.org/10.1037/1040-3590.4.1.26.

González, J. et al. (August 15, 2006). "Reading cinnamon activates olfactory brain regions." *NeuroImage* 32(2): 906–912. https://pubmed.ncbi.nlm.nih.gov/16651007/.

Granneman, J. (March 4, 2015). "Introverts' and extroverts' brains really are different, according to science." *Science*. Retrieved from https://introvertdear.com/news/introverts-and-extroverts-brains-really-are-different-according-to-science/.

Harir, A. et al. (July 19, 2002). "Serotonin transporter genetic variation and the response of the human amygdala." *Science* 297(5580), 400–403.

Hegarty, A. (August 18, 2011). "Horrible bosses living up to name." *The Advertiser*. https://www.adelaidenow.com.au/news/horrible-bosses-living-up-to-name/news-story/95eb2c8d9efcda530d1faf9b-7da8863f.

Hersey, P., & Blanchard, K. H. (1969). "Life cycle theory of leadership." *Training & Development Journal* 23(5): 26–34.

Hewlett Packard Enterprise. "Our Culture: Empowering our people." https://www.hpe.com/us/en/about/diversity/culture.html#:~:text=Our%20culture%20is%20what%20defines,and%20always%20putting%20partnerships%20first.

Howell, J. (2012). *Becoming Conscious: The Enneagram's Forgotten Passageway*. Balboa Press. 203.

Hurlemann, R. et al. (April 7, 2010). "Oxytocin enhances amygdala-dependent, socially reinforced learning and emotional empathy in humans." *Journal of Neuroscience* 14: 4999–5007.

Johnson-Laird, P. (May 8, 2012). "Mental models and cognitive change." *Journal of Cognitive Psychology* 25(2): 131–138.

Kleinman, P. (2012). *Psych101*. F+W Media.

Lin, P. et al (February 27, 2013). "Oxytocin Increases the Influence of Public Service Advertisements." *PLOS One*. Retrieved from https://journals.plos.org/plosone/article?id=10.1371/journal.pone.0056934.

MacGill, M. (September 4, 2017). "What is the link between love and oxytocin?" *Medical News Today*. Retrieved from https://www.medicalnewstoday.com/articles/275795.php.

MacLean, P. (January 31, 1990). *The Triune Brain in Evolution: Role in Paleocerebral Functions*. New York: Plenum Press. 9.

Mahoney, M. (January 13, 2003). "The subconscious mind of the consumer (and how to reach it)." Retrieved from https://hbswk.hbs.edu/item/the-subconscious-mind-of-the-consumer-and-how-to-reach-it.

Mattone, J. (April 13, 2013). *Intelligent Leadership: What You Need to Know to Unlock Your Full Potential*. New York: AMACOM (HarperCollins), 82–100.

News.com.au (November 16, 2011). "Two-thirds of Australians have a 'horrible' or 'average' boss, survey finds." Retrieved from https://www.news.com.au/finance/work/survey-finds-two-thirds-of-responders-have-a-horrible-or-average-boss/news-story/7667099c6e13f73c9644a0f53555933a.

Ouimet, M. (November 15, 2012). "The Real Productivity-Killer: Jerks." *Inc.* Retrieved from www.inc.com/maeghan-ouimet/real-cost-bad-bosses.html.

Schawbel, D. (January 23, 2012). "Hire For Attitude." *Forbes*. https://www.forbes.com/sites/danschawbel/2012/01/23/89-of-new-hires-fail-because-of-their-attitude/?sh=15e6571c137a.

Schwartz, J. & Thomson, J. (December 5, 2016). "The Neuroscience of Strategic Leadership." strategy + business, Issue 87. Retrieved from https://www.strategy-business.com/article/The-Neuroscience-of-Strategic-Leadership?gko=d196c.

ScienceDaily (2017). "Neocortex." Retrieved from https://www.sciencedaily.com/terms/neocortex.htm.

Sendjaya, S. & Sarros, J. (Fall 2002). "Servant leadership: Its origin, development, and application in organizations." *Journal of Leadership & Organizational Studies* 9 (2): 57.

Smith, J. (June 6, 2016). "Here's why workplace stress is costing employers $300 billion a year." Business Insider. https://www.businessinsider.com/how-stress-at-work-is-costing-employers-300-billion-a-year-2016-6.

Snyder, B. (April 2, 2015). "Half of us have quit our job because of a bad boss." *Fortune.* https://fortune.com/2015/04/02/quit-reasons/.

Society for Human Resource Management (April 28, 2015). "Employee job satisfaction and engagement: Optimizing organizational culture for success." Retrieved from https://www.shrm.org/hr-today/trends-and-forecasting/research-and-surveys/pages/jobsatisfaction-and-engagement-rreport-optimizing-organizational-culture-for-success.aspx.

Speer, N. et al (August 2009). "Reading Stories Activates Neural Representations of Visual and Motor Experiences." *Psychological Science* 20 (8): 989–999. Retrieved from https://www.ncbi.nlm.nih.gov/pmc/articles/PMC2819196/.

Thomas, T. (2016). *Who Do You Think You Are?: Understanding Your personality from the Inside Out.* New York: Morgan James Publishing, 173–178.

Todd, R. et al (April 22, 2015). "Neurogenetic variations in norepinephrine availability enhance perceptual vividness." *Journal of Neuroscience* 35(16): 6506–6516. doi:10.1523/JNEUROSCI.4489-14.2015.

University of British Columbia (May 7, 2015). "How your brain reacts to emotional information is influenced by your genes." *ScienceDaily*. Retrieved from www.sciencedaily.com/releases/2015/05/150507135919.htm.

Vermeulen, F. (July 2, 2012). "Strategy is the story: A good leader should be a good storyteller." London Business School. Retrieved from https://www.london.edu/faculty-and-research/lbsr/strategy-is-the-story.

Waldman, D., Balthazard, P., & Peterson, S. (February 2011). "Leadership and Neuroscience: Can We Revolutionize the Way That Inspirational Leaders Are Identified and Developed?" *Academy of Management Perspectives* 25(1): 60–74.

Weber, L. (2015). "What do workers want from the boss?" *Wall Street Journal*. Retrieved from https://blogs.wsj.com/atwork/2015/04/02/what-do-workers-want-from-the-boss/?mod=e2tw.

Winerman, L. (October 2005). "The mind's mirror: A new type of neuron—called a mirror neuron—could help explain how we learn through mimicry and why we empathize with others." *Monitor* 36(9): 48.

Wolfgang, J. (2018). Quotation, *Goodreads*, https://www.goodreads.com/quotes/122348-he-who-cannot-draw-on-three-thousand-years-is-living.

Zak, P. (February 2017). "The Neuroscience of Trust." *Harvard Business Review*. Retrieved from https://hbr.org/2017/01/the-neuroscience-of-trust.

Zak, P. (January 17, 2017). *Trust Factor: The Science of Creating High-Performance Companies*. New York: AMACOM (HarperCollins), 300.

ABOUT THE AUTHOR

William Craig Reed is the *New York Times* bestselling author of several award-winning books including *The 7 Secrets of Neuron Leadership* (Wiley), *Red November* (HarperCollins), and *Spies of the Deep: The Untold Truth About the Most Terrifying Incident in Submarine Naval History and How Putin Used The Tragedy To Ignite a New Cold War* (Post Hill Press). Reed served as a U.S. Navy submariner and diver during the Cold War and earned commendations for completing secret missions, some in concert with SEAL Team One. Reed serves on the board of directors for RemotelyMe, the leading company in ChatGPT neuroscience-personalization for recruiting and sales. He holds an MBA, certifications in marketing and leadership, and a neuroscience certification from Harvard University. Reed has launched three successful startups acquired by Intel, NetApp, and Helius, and helped a dozen other firms achieve similar success. As an executive consultant, Reed's clients have included Avnet, Booz Allen Hamilton, Cisco, HP, Oracle, SAP, Visa, and many others